Rudolf Herz

Marcel Duchamp. La Patte

Rudolf Herz

Marcel Duchamp
La Patte

KERBER ART

INHALT

CONTENTS

Heinrich Hoffmann: Marcel Duchamp, 1912

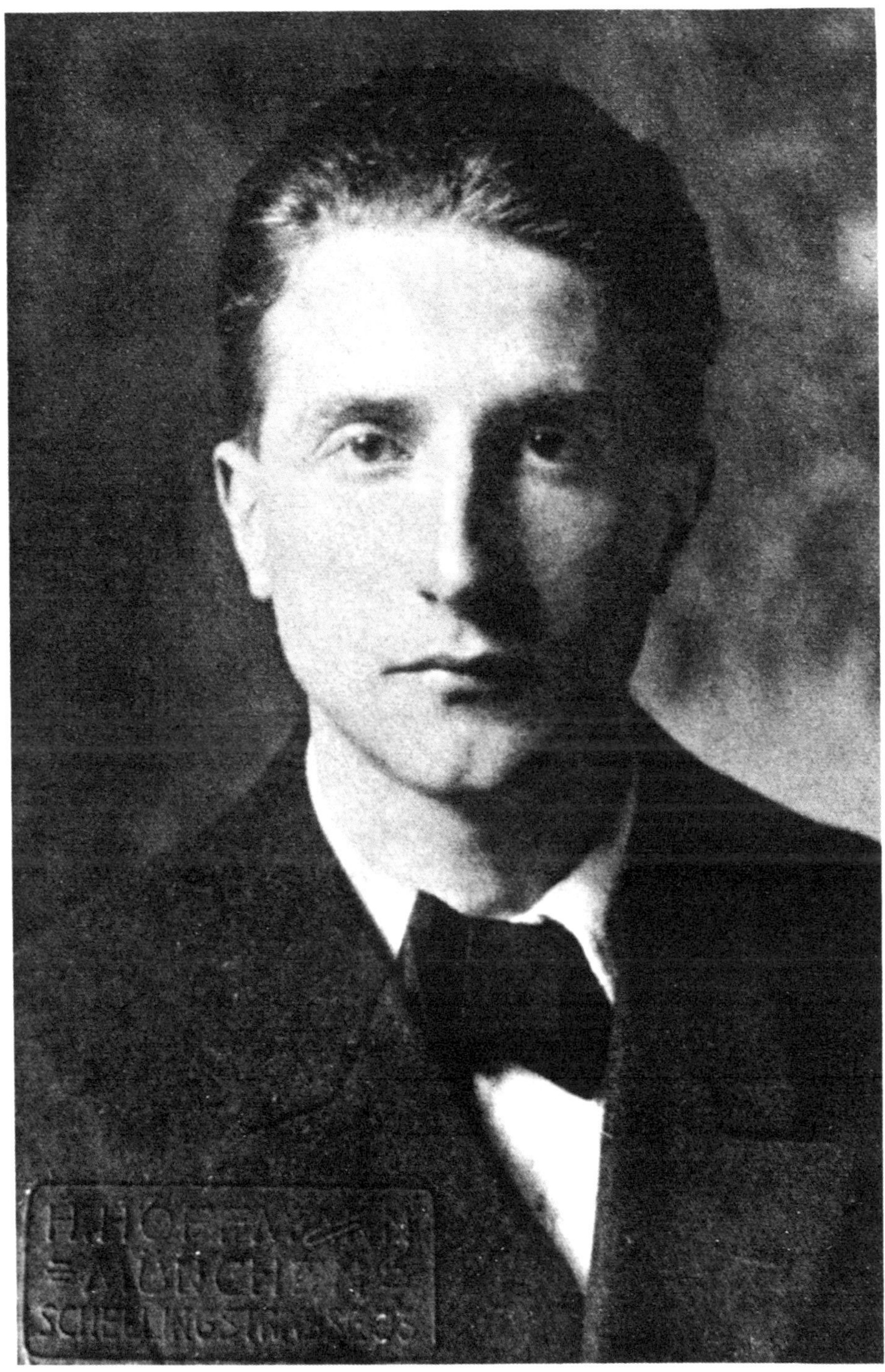

H. HOFFMANN
MÜNCHEN
SCHELLINGSTRASSE 33

PHILIPP NORMAN JOHN / MARIE-JOSÉ SONDEIJKER

Paris-München-Paris

Von Marcel Duchamps Werk hat sich Rudolf Herz mehrfach inspirieren lassen. Über Jahre hinweg hat er die Auseinandersetzung mit diesem Werk gesucht und ästhetische Experimente gewagt: provokante Rauminstallationen, eine skulpturale Setzung im öffentlichen Raum, Schriftzüge aus weißem Rauch am Himmel. Er hat historisch-kritische Forschungen angestellt, um einen neuen Zugang zu eröffnen. Damit steht er nicht allein; auch Künstler wie Serge Stauffer oder Stefan Banz haben Duchamps Wege erkundet.

Den Anstoß gab eine wenig bekannte Portraitaufnahme von Duchamp, auf die Herz während seines Kunststudiums stieß. Sie entstand im Sommer 1912, als sich der 25-jährige Duchamp drei Monate in München aufhielt. In einer ersten künstlerischen Operation mit diesem Porträt stellte Herz großformatige Siebdrucke her und kontrastierte sie in der schachbrettartigen Rauminstallation ›Zugzwang‹ (Kunstverein Ruhr, Essen 1996, The Jewish Museum, New York City 2002 und anderenorts) mit gleich großen Siebdrucken eines Porträts von Adolf Hitler. Die Installation erzeugt ein nicht leicht auflösbares Beziehungsgeflecht und stellt unser Bildverständnis auf die Probe. Dass beide Porträts von Hitlers späterem ›Hoffotografen‹ Hoffmann stammen, ist für Herz nicht viel mehr als Zufall.

Zeit seines Lebens hat Duchamp versucht, die Spuren seines Aufenthalts in München zu verwischen, auch wenn diese Monate den wohl folgenreichsten Abschnitt seiner künstlerischen Biografie darstellen. In dem detektivisch angelegten Projekt ›Marcel Duchamp. Le Mystère de Munich‹ (Architekturmuseum der TU München 2012) hat Rudolf Herz die Hintergründe detailliert ausgeleuchtet.

In den Mittelpunkt rückte die Münchner Wohnung, in der Duchamp 1912 zur Untermiete wohnte – für Herz die Wiege der konzeptuellen Kunst.

Entscheidend für Duchamps Münchner Zeit war die spezifische Erfahrung moderner Technik, die sein Kunstverständnis radikal verändern und zum Abschied von der Malerei führen sollte. Und sie befreite ihn vom Bemühen um eine persönliche Handschrift, die er mit einer französischen Umschreibung ›la patte‹ – Pranke, Tatze – nannte. Dieser neuen Auffassung folgten alsbald die Readymades und das später in Angriff genommene Meisterwerk ›Das Große Glas‹. Duchamps Portrait, so die These von Rudolf Herz, nimmt diese Entwicklung freilich schon vorweg.

Auf Duchamps Absage an ›la patte‹, die künstlerische Handschrift, antwortete Herz mit einer Aktion in entgegengesetzter Richtung. Er beauftragte 17 Pariser Straßenkünstler, Kopien des Münchner Portraits anzufertigen. Er ließ ihnen vollkommen freie Hand und war neugierig, wie die Interpretationen ausfallen würden. In der Tat überraschen die Zeichnungen mit ihrem stilistischen Spektrum und der Vielfalt der entworfenen Persönlichkeitsprofile.

Wir freuen uns, unter dem Titel ›Marcel Duchamp. La Patte‹ die Ergebnisse der Pariser Aktion zeigen und erstmals die komplette Serie der Zeichnungen ausstellen zu können. Diese Publikation gibt die Portraitserie wieder, begleitet von drei Texten, die verschiedene Aspekte des Projekts und seiner Entstehung herausarbeiten.

RUDOLF HERZ

Marcel Duchamp. La Patte

Im Zuge meiner Recherchen zu Marcel Duchamp bin ich öfter nach Paris gefahren und fing auch an, die Straßenmaler auf dem Montmartre zu besuchen. Irgendwann bat ich sie, Kopien des Portraits anzufertigen, das Marcel Duchamp 1912 während seines München-Aufenthalts vom Fotografen Heinrich Hoffmann hatte aufnehmen lassen. 17 Zeichnungen sind auf diese Weise entstanden, mit sehr unterschiedlicher Handschrift. Unter dem Titel ›Marcel Duchamp. La Patte‹ habe ich sie zusammengefasst.

Die Pariser Straßenkünstler wollten genau wissen, wessen Bild ich ihnen präsentierte. Duchamp war nicht allen bekannt. Wenn ich die Zeichnungen dann später Freunden und Kollegen zeigte, war die spontane Reaktion ein vergleichendes Bewerten: Dieses Portrait trifft Duchamp doch viel besser als jenes, und das da, das ist ja komisch! Jenseits von Qualitätsfragen finde ich interessant, welch konträre Auffassungen und Persönlichkeitsprofile die Zeichnungen entwerfen und welche charakterlichen und sozialen Mutmaßungen sie hervorrufen. Da gibt es den androgynen Schüler, den Cowboy, den feinsinnigen Intellektuellen, den mexikanischen Drogenbaron oder den Absinth-Konsumenten im Delirium. Genau diese Summe der interpretatorischen Möglichkeiten finde ich bemerkenswert.

Seit ich Duchamps Portraitaufnahme zum ersten Mal zu Gesicht bekam, hat sie mich nicht mehr losgelassen. Sie hat mich angespornt, sehr verschiedene Vorhaben zu verfolgen. ›Marcel Duchamp. La Patte‹ kreist auf ironische Art und Weise um das Phänomen der künstlerischen Handschrift. Zu dem Zeitpunkt, als sich Duchamp von Hoffmann fotografieren ließ, stand er vor der Frage, wie er es in Zukunft in seiner Kunst mit ebendieser Handschrift halten sollte. Meine

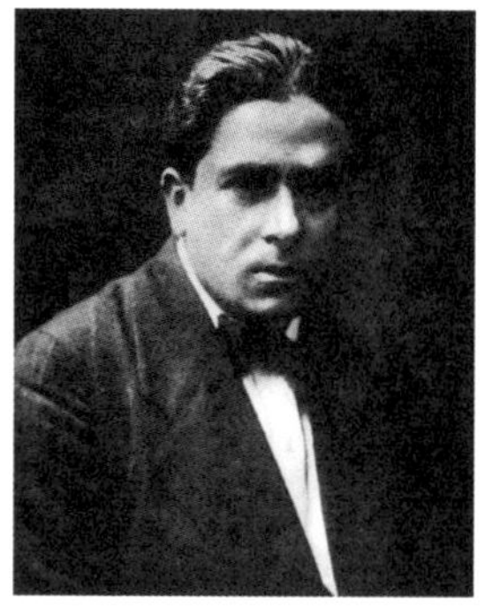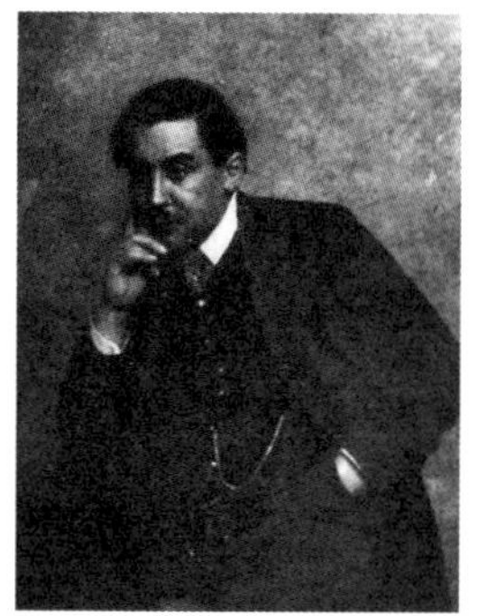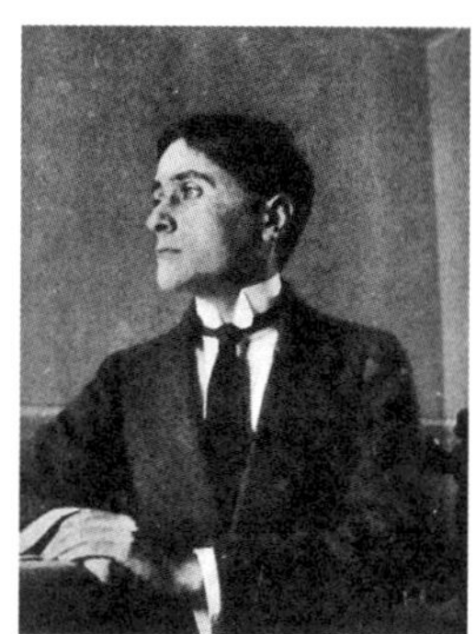

Francis Picabia, Albert Gleizes, Jean Metzinger, in: Guillaume Apollinaire: Méditations Esthétiques. Les Peintres Cubistes, Paris 1913

These ist: Seine baldige Abkehr von ihr spiegelt sich schon in der Auffassung dieser Portraitfotografie wider. Diese Aufnahme verweist also auf die kommende Entwicklung.

Ich hatte mich gefragt: Warum ließ sich Duchamp, als ihn Guillaume Apollinaire im Sommer 1912 um ein Portrait für sein Kubismus-Buch bat, ausgerechnet auf diese sterile Art und Weise ablichten? Er wirkt gelangweilt, mit dem erstarrten Gesicht einer Statue oder Porzellanpuppe, sucht nicht nach intensivem Augenkontakt: Er nimmt die Haltung der Indifferenz ein, die er später als künstlerische Haltung propagieren sollte.

Für die damals übliche Atelierfotografie, wie auch für damalige Künstlerbildnisse, ist das Portrait ziemlich untypisch. Das sieht man, wenn man es mit den sehr individuellen Portraitaufnahmen der Künstlerkollegen Francis Picabia, Albert Gleizes und Jean Metzinger in Apollinaires Buch vergleicht, die allesamt malerische Valeurs und Manipulationen bemühen und der zeitgenössischen Kunstfotografie zuzuordnen sind. Davon will sich Duchamp ganz offenkundig abgrenzen. Das Resultat der Portraitsitzung bei Hoffmann erinnert an administrative Pass- und Polizeifotografien, die keine psychologische Einfühlung kennen, sich nicht um Emotion und individuellen Ausdruck kümmern: anatomische Datenblätter, die die Person als bloßes Objekt behandeln. Diese kühle Herangehensweise, diese technisch-maschinelle Auffassung ist eine künstlerische Errungenschaft, eine Methode, die Duchamp seinem Münchner Aufenthalt verdankt.

Konkret waren es die Seherlebnisse im Deutschen Museum und auf einer Industriemesse, die ihn dazu geführt haben dürften. Nicht zuletzt aber wird der enge Kontakt zu seinen jungen Vermietern in der Barer Straße 65 eine Rolle gespielt haben: eine Schneiderin und ein versierter Ingenieur bei der Lokomotivenfabrik Maffei, der zuvor die Abteilung für technische Zeichnungen im Oldenbourg Verlag leitete. Das 12-Quadratmeter-Zimmer in dieser Wohnung mit Blick auf die Barer Straße, das Duchamp über eine Zeitungsannonce fand, wurde zum Zentrum seiner neuen Erkenntnisse und seines Schaffens während des dreimonatigen Aufenthalts in München. Dieses Zimmer, behaupte ich, ist die Wiege der konzeptuellen Kunst! Ich verwandelte die Wohnung zusammen mit dem Architekten Peter Ottmann in eine Großskulptur, im Maßstab 1:1, kippte sie um 90 Grad und stellte sie vor die Alte Pinakothek.

Duchamps neue Auffassung findet sich alsbald in der Entwicklung der Ready-mades und in der Konzeption des ›Großen Glases‹ wieder. Rückblickend erklärte

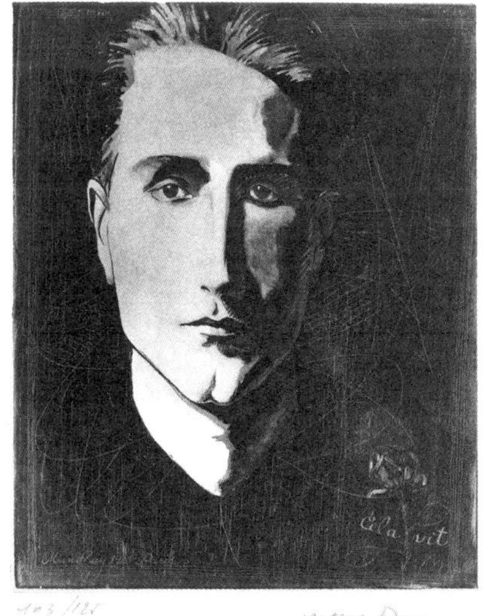

Man Ray: Cela vit, Marcel Duchamp

13

er, dass es nicht einmal die Bewegungsdarstellung des spektakulären Werks ›Akt, eine Treppe herabsteigend‹ war, die für ihn »ein Fenster zu etwas anderem hin geöffnet« hätte, sondern technische Darstellungen und technische Zeichnungen. Seine Polemik gegen die »retinale Malerei«, den Augeneindruck, ging einher mit der Polemik gegen die »künstlerische Handschrift«. Zu seinem Biografen Calvin Tomkins sagt er 1965: »Der springende Punkt war, meine Hand zu vergessen.« Und an anderer Stelle: »Auf Französisch gibt es einen alten Ausdruck: ›la patte‹, was den Pinselstrich eines Künstlers, seinen persönlichen Stil, seine ›Tatze‹ bezeichnet. Ich wollte loskommen von ›la patte‹ und von dieser ganzen retinalen Malerei ... ab 1912 beschloss ich aufzuhören, ein Maler im professionellen Sinne zu sein.«

Duchamps Portraitaufnahme ist ohne »Tatze«, aufs Äußerste reduziert. Sie enthält ein Minimum an Angaben zur Person, sie ist die radikale Negation eines persönlichen Stils. Duchamp wendet seine neue Auffassung also bereits 1912 auf sein eigenes Portrait an. Es ist so etwas wie der Versuch eines fotografischen Nullpunkts, befreit von körpersprachlichen und ästhetischen Zutaten. Man darf annehmen, dass die gestalterische Entscheidung allein bei Duchamp lag und Hoffmann nur die Kamera zu bedienen hatte. Insofern könnte man auch von Duchamps Selbstportrait sprechen.

In ›Marcel Duchamp. La Patte‹ fallen die Pariser Zeichner gleichsam über Duchamp her und drücken seiner trockenen Portraitaufnahme unübersehbar ihre »Tatze«, auf. Mein Projekt konterkariert Duchamps ursprünglichen Ansatz, und in der Folge bringen die Künstler nicht nur ihre je eigene ›Tatze‹ zur Geltung, sondern individualisieren Duchamp in vielfältiger Weise. Und in der Summe ihrer Portraits eröffnet sich ein experimentelles Rollenspiel voller Kontraste. Und hier gilt nicht ›entweder oder‹, sondern ›sowohl als auch‹. Man könnte in den einzelnen Zeichnungen auch Standbilder eines morphologisch konzipierten Films sehen und sich ein filmisches Schauspiel wechselnder Identitäten vorstellen.

Die Pariser Zeichnungen stehen nicht allein da. Bereits 1923 hat Man Ray Hoffmanns Duchamp-Aufnahme zur Grundlage der Aquatinta-Radierung ›Cela Vit‹ gemacht. Er verhalf Duchamp zu einem suggestiv-dramatischen Aussehen; der junge Mann könnte Schauspieler oder Filmstar sein. Man Ray fotografierte auch Duchamps Selbstinszenierung als androgynes Alter Ego ›Rrose Sélavy‹, ein Pseudonym, das ihm bis dahin nur als Signatur diente. Duchamp inszenierte sich als ältere, melancholisch wirkende Frau. Er spielte mit der traditionellen Rollenverteilung und dem heteronomen Geschlechterverhältnis.

Die Verwandlung des eigenen Ichs ließ Duchamp nicht mehr los. Er entwickelte daraus eine künstlerische Strategie und nahm sogar seine eigene Alterung vorweg, als er sich 1945 in New York mit der Fotografie ›at the age of 85‹ als greisenhafter Künstler-Philosoph in Szene setzte. Damals war er gerade 58 Jahre alt. Er wusste genau, wie sein Gesicht maskenbildnerisch und fotografisch zu manipulieren war, um überzeugende Wirkung eines fiktionalen Bildes zu erreichen.

Duchamp wollte weder sich als Person noch seine künstlerische Auffassung festlegen. Er verweigerte sich jeglicher Identität, die ihn einengen könnte. Er setzte aufs Experiment und wollte keinen Stil kreieren. Damit provoziert er uns bis heute – das liegt in der Logik seiner Idee künstlerischer Freiheit.

Mein großer Dank gilt den Pariser Straßenmalern und Straßenmalerinnen.

ANTJE VON GRAEVENITZ

Marcel Duchamps
›Portrait-Objekt‹, wiederbelebt

Welche Verführung geht von einem Pariser Straßenkünstler aus, sich von ihm zeichnen zu lassen! Zu gern möchte man wissen, wie er einen wahrnimmt und darstellt. Wird sein Portrait so ähnlich, wie ich mich kenne, oder ganz anders? Fokussiert es einen unbekannten oder lieber verborgen gehaltenen Charakterzug, den nur dieser Zeichner »hervorholt«?

Lange bevor es Fotoportraits gab, waren gezeichnete Wiedergaben eines Gesichtes Gang und Gäbe. Wer es naturgetreu zu zeichnen verstand, war zumeist erfolgreich. Dabei hoffte ein Modell nicht nur, endlich zu sehen, wie es aussah, womöglich anders als im Spiegel. Sondern es wünschte sich auch, erkennen zu können, wie andere (als pars pro toto für jeden) es wahrnehmen würden, denn eine Interpretation floss ganz selbstverständlich über die zeichnende Hand in die Linien mit ein. Zudem war der Umstand willkommen, dass durch die Zeichnung der Augenblick des Lebens überdauern könnte: jung und vielleicht schön oder ausdrucksstark und womöglich weise. Man wollte sich überraschen lassen: Welche Identität hatte darin das eigene Ich? Geduldig nahm man dafür als Modell vor dem Zeichner Platz – ob zu Hause, im Atelier oder auf der Straße – und wartete auf das Ergebnis. Dieses künstlerische Prozedere war lange Zeit keine Selbstverständlichkeit. Offiziell bürgerte es sich zumindest erst seit dem Ende des Mittelalters ein, als das ›Ich‹ endlich im Bild Eingang fand. Gezeichnet diente es bald einer Sammlung, als Unterpfand eines Vertrages, als Steckbrief oder auch als Werbung für einen Ehevertrag, wenn die tatsächliche Braut noch weit entfernt lebte und ihr Gesichtsbild beim eventuellen Bräutigam schon Gefühle auslösen sollte. Also wurde ein Bild des Gesichts ein wichtiges ›Ding‹. Welche Revolution das war, ist im Selfie-Zeitalter nur schwer vorstellbar.

Gleiches Erstaunen weckt wohl heute die Geschichte der Portraitfotografie, denn einige Jahre nach der Erfindung (1826) der fotografischen Technik war es ab 1839 zunächst ein Privileg der Reichen, um sich in langen Sitzungen vor der Kamera umständlich ablichten zu lassen. Auch dies wurde ein ›Ding‹: Man handelte damit als ›carte de visite‹ für soziale Aufmerksamkeit und gegen das Vergessen. Die betroffenen Modelle betrachteten wohl staunend das abgelichtete Ergebnis: zumeist als ernst und starr blickendes Gesicht, von dem sie meinten, es halte das echte, das wahre Leben im Bild fest, viel realistischer als jede Zeichnung. Dass auch ein Fotograf seine Interpretation vom Modell einbrächte, blieb lange unbesprochen. Ein Foto gäbe die Wirklichkeit exakt wieder, so glaubte man. Sie entspräche doch einer genauen Identität des Gesichtes, so jedenfalls nahmen es Mediziner von fotografierten Hysterikern an, Polizisten von Fotos angeblicher und überführter krimineller Personen, Zollbeamte von Passfotos der Reisenden und Ethnologen von Serien-Aufnahmen (kolonialisierter) Außer-Europäern zwecks vermeintlicher wissenschaftlicher Untersuchungen. Sie alle glaubten bei ihren Foto-Sammlungen von direkten Gesichtsaufnahmen immer an im Bild materialisierte Realien der Betroffenen.

In Belgien wollte man schon ab 1870 solche sachlichen Gesichtsaufnahmen für Heimatlose, Vagabunden, Bettler und Verdächtige einführen, in Frankreich erst, nachdem Alphonse Bertillon 1882 die ›photographie signalétique‹ zur behördlichen Erfassung von Identitäten vorgeschlagen hatte. Er musste dennoch einräumen, dass damit die Bedürfnisse letztlich nicht zu erfüllen waren, weil Identität erst durch Verschiedenheit im Aussehen entsteht, wie Hans Belting in seinem Buch ›Faces. Eine Geschichte des Gesichtes‹ (2013) anschaulich schildert. Je versteinerter deren Blick in die Kamera wirkte, je maskenhafter die Vorderseite erschien, je deutlicher der Ohrenansatz zu sehen blieb, desto dinghafter erschien ein Mensch auf der Gesichtsaufnahme. Dinghaft – und also wie zu haben und zu handhaben – erschien somit die Identität jedes Menschen, ganz und gar eingeklemmt in den engen Rahmen der Gesichtsaufnahme.

Dinghaft ist hier Stichwort und zugleich Hypothese. Denn warum sollte sich Marcel Duchamp von dem Fotografen Heinrich Hoffmann 1912 bei seinem

Aufenthalt in München für ein Buch von Guillaume Apollinaire gerade im Passfoto-Stil mit versteinertem Gesichtsausdruck ablichten lassen, er, der doch mit seinem Bild ›Akt, eine Treppe herabsteigend‹ 1912 Bewegung darstellte? Der genug zu haben schien von allen liegenden oder sitzenden Aktdarstellungen der Vergangenheit? Warum also hatte Duchamp in seinem Konterfei keinerlei Ausdruck als Zeichen zumindest innerer Bewegung in sein Portrait hineinbringen wollen? Warum wollte er jegliche psychische Identität vermeiden und nur eine formale Identität festgelegt haben? Immerhin sieht er einen mit kleinen, etwas ungleichen Augen im langen Gesicht mit entsprechender Nase und Grübchen im Kinn an. Sein Gesicht ›gibt nicht mehr her‹. Soweit zumindest gleicht es keinem anderen. Aber die starre Vorderansicht des Gesichtes ›spricht Bände‹: Polizeifotos waren erst etwas mehr als 20 Jahre lang in Frankreich üblich und hatten so als stilistische Kategorie wohl noch einige »Aktualität«. Wollte Duchamp sich Hysterikern, Kriminellen, Reisenden oder Außereuropäern angleichen? Wollte er, der zur Intention seiner Readymades (beispielsweise zum ›Flaschentrockner‹, ›Urinoir‹ und ›Hat-Rack‹) bis an sein Lebensende erklärte, er sei bei der Auswahl vollkommen »gleichgültig« gewesen, wollte er diese Indifferenz schon bei seinem Portraitfoto von 1912 in Anspruch nehmen? Es wurde sein zentrales Anliegen, sein wichtigstes theoretisches Ziel.

Ging es ihm nicht um sein Ebenbild? Wollte er kein Foto, sondern ein ›Foto-Ding‹ erzeugt haben? Eines, das ein Fotograf einfach nach banalen offiziellen Regeln produzieren konnte? Immerhin zeigte er sich später im Foto-Steckbrief eines Kriminellen (1923 als ›Wanted‹) oder auch 1921 als Dame ›Rrose Sélavy‹ auf Parfumfläschchen ›Belle Haleine‹ und gab somit zu verstehen, an keinerlei Identität eines Marcel Duchamp interessiert zu sein, sondern eher an einer fiktiven Doppel-Identität, die der eigenen den Grund unter den Füßen wegfegte. Fotografierte Realität: Gab es die überhaupt? Wenn es denn zu anderen Aufnahmen von Duchamp kam, zum Beispiel beim Schachspielen oder mit Freunden, dann nicht von ihm formal (mit)inszeniert. Mit anderen Worten: Diese Argumentation führt zur Annahme, dass Objekthaftigkeit und Indifferenz dem Fotografen Hoffmann als Duchamps Intention vorgegeben wurden.

Zu all diesen Überlegungen kommt auch Rudolf Herz. Dennoch gab er sich mit Duchamps Verdikt – als das man es doch wohl bezeichnen kann – nicht zufrieden.

Er versuchte in den Jahren von 2012 bis 2017 (im Intervall von hundert Jahren) den umgekehrten Weg zu gehen, also nicht die Entwicklung von der individuellen Portraitzeichnung zur identitätslosen Portrait-Fotografie an einem Beispiel nachzuzeichnen, sondern von ihr zurück zur Portraitzeichnung: Siebzehnmal löste sich nun die Indifferenz in Duchamp Konterfei in Interpretationen auf. Ob diese Aufgabe für diese Straßenkünstler ungewöhnlich war und sie vielleicht sogar verunsicherte, ist hier nicht die Frage, sondern wie sahen sie Duchamp? Versuchten sie sich in das Gesicht hineinzudenken? Wie erzeugten sie in der Quasi-Fotoübertragung ein lebendiges Gesicht? Entdeckten sie darin etwas, was Duchamp im Foto-Ding versteckt hatte?

Phantasie zu zeigen gehörte nicht zu ihrer Aufgabe, eher vor allem Ähnlichkeit zu erzeugen. Auf jeder Zeichnung liegt überraschenderweise dennoch ein neuer Akzent: Duchamps Kopf wurde beispielsweise auf einmal geringfügig geneigt wiedergegeben, die Lippen ein wenig lächelnd, als würde er zuhören und sich über das Gehörte amüsieren. So könnte er in Wahrheit ausgesehen haben. Dann wieder blickt er als Gezeichneter etwas traurig oder nachdenklich (und in der Tat scheint Duchamp um 1912 etliche enttäuschende Momente erfahren haben, wie Rudolf Herz in seinem Buch ›Marcel Duchamp. Le Mystère de Munich‹ über diese Periode erzählte. Wusste der Pariser Zeichner davon?). Duchamps Stirn, die auf seinem Foto nicht ganz gleichmäßig symmetrisch abgebildet ist, wurde von manchem Zeichner genau beobachtet und nun so stark akzentuiert, dass sie sich zur unschönen Auffälligkeit entpuppt. Oder aber Duchamp sieht auf einmal verträumt aus, ganz wie ein junger Romantiker, leidend wie Goethes alter ego »Werther«.

Vielleicht war es damals in München seine zweite, kaum vorgezeigte Seite, die ein Zeichner – ob unbewusst oder nicht – in Duchamps Gesicht erkannte? Manch anderer gibt ihn wiederum sportlich wieder, entweder mit prall gefüllten Backen, die sogar farbig hervorleuchten, oder mit scharfem und verstärkt konturiertem Kiefer und verdickten Lippen. Ob Duchamp je Sport betrieben hat, blieb im Vergessen. Dann wieder blickt der Gezeichnete fragend nach vorn oder nach unten und erscheint so gut gekleidet wie ein junger aufstrebender Bankier. Auch trotzig kann dieses Gesicht nun seinen Mund geschürzt vorzeigen oder im Gegenteil: mit etwas eingezogenem Mund feinsinnig, in sich gekehrt und verletzlich wirken. Wer Duchamps Biographie und seine künstlerischen Intentionen kennt, wird sich beides vorstellen können. Anscheinend waren manche der Zeichner in dieser Hinsicht gute Beobachter. Formal versuchten sie ihre eigenen Fähigkeiten mit konturierten oder verwischten Strichen anzuwenden, um Dunkelheiten zu erzeugen, um nach üblichem Gusto gebogene, gekreuzte oder vertikale Schraffierungen einzubringen oder sich an die vorgegebenen Hell-Dunkel-Details auf dem Foto zu halten, indem sie das Gesicht zum Beispiel zu einem Viertel verschatteten, es insgesamt aber im Licht leuchten ließen. Einmal deutet man sogar hinter Duchamps Kopf eine winzige Aureole an.

Der eine Zeichner scheint sein Können geschickter einzusetzen als der andere, aber allen insgesamt gleich ist doch der Versuch, ein fast erstarrt wirkendes Image mit minimalen Mitteln zeichnerisch zu verlebendigen. Ähnlichkeit zu erzeugen schien gerade nicht ihr Ziel, sondern den Dargestellten in die Gegenwart zu holen. Damit geben uns die siebzehn Versuche Duchamp als Menschen zurück, der sich uns Betrachtenden offensichtlich zu entziehen gedachte. Im Grunde jedoch sind die siebzehn Abzeichnungen so unterschiedlich, dass sich die verlebendigte Identität doch wieder in Nicht-Identität verflüchtigt. Das passt zu Duchamps Vorliebe für Widersprüche.

Vielleicht wäre es Duchamp also durchaus recht gewesen, dass sein Gesicht etwa ein Jahrhundert später von anonymen Straßenzeichnern siebzehn Mal neu gesehen wurde. Auch ein Fotograf wie Hoffmann war immerhin ein ›Mitarbeiter‹ am Foto-Ding. Und schließlich erklärte Duchamp in seinem Aspen-Vortrag 1957, der Betrachter mache das Werk … In diesem Falle waren es sogar siebzehn, die zeichneten, was sie zu sehen glaubten. Man erkennt all die Mühen der Straßenzeichner, dem sterilen Foto Duchamps Leben einzuhauchen. Gerade dadurch wird es als früher Versuch eines identitätsentfremdeten Readymades verständlich.

PHILIPP NORMAN JOHN

Das Selbstporträt als Befreiungsmoment bei Marcel Duchamp

Ein Portraitfoto, 17 unbekannte Straßenmaler von heute und eine biografische Lücke im Leben des Künstlers Marcel Duchamp. Der indes verkörpert eine der einflussreichsten Positionen der Moderne. Dieser spannungsgeladene Ausgangspunkt weist Aspekte eines kunsthistorischen Dramas auf, auf das der Münchener Künstler Rudolf Herz in seiner Aktion aufmerksam macht und deren Ergebnisse in diese Ausstellung münden und hier veröffentlicht sind.

Der Ort, den Rudolf Herz für seine Aktion gewählt hat, ist nicht zufällig gewählt. Denn es war die Stadt Paris, die Wiege der modernen Malerei, die Marcel Duchamp im Sommer 1912 verlassen hatte, um zu den Auseinandersetzungen um den ›richtigen‹ Weg der Malerei auf Distanz zu gehen, den der Kubismus und viele andere Ismen zu dieser Zeit für sich beanspruchten. In diese Szene war Duchamp tief verstrickt. Einerseits hatte er über den Salon d'Automne bereits Bilder verkauft, andererseits wurde sein ›Akt, eine Treppe herabsteigend‹ selbst von seinen Freunden abgelehnt, woraufhin er das Bild aus dem Salon des Indépendants eigenhändig entfernte. Apollinaire hatte einen anderen seiner Akte »extrem hässlich« genannt. Das klingt nicht gut, muss aber im Rahmen der damaligen Auseinandersetzung um aktuelle Malerei nicht unbedingt despektierlich gemeint sein, zumal selbiger Autor Duchamp ja in seine Anthologie ›Les Peintres Cubistes‹ aufnahm und ihn am Ende sogar mit dem Satz nobilitierte, »Es wird vielleicht einem Künstler vorbehalten sein, der so frei von ästhetischen Bedenken ist und so auf Energie bedacht wie Marcel Duchamp, die Kunst und das Volk wieder miteinander zu versöhnen.«[1] Im Übrigen war Duchamp in die

Frau seines Freundes Francis Picabia verliebt und hatte einer verheirateten Frau
ein Kind gemacht ... Da kam die Einladung eines Malerfreundes nach München
gerade recht.

Duchamp ging auf Distanz: zur Pariser Kunstszene, zu privaten Verstrickungen,
zum Kubismus, zur Malerei insgesamt ... und fand in München zu sich selbst. In
Duchamps eigenen Worten: »Mein Aufenthalt in München war der Ort meiner
völligen Befreiung.«

Rudolf Herz vermutet, dass Hoffmanns Portrait ein Schlüssel zu diesem
entscheidenden Moment sein muss, weil das Selbstportrait seit je her als
Dokument für die künstlerische Haltung des Portraitierten gegolten hat. Das in der
Münchener Pinakothek hängende Selbstbildnis Dürers von 1500, auf das Herz in
seiner Publikation ›Marcel Duchamp. Le Mystère de Munich‹ (2012) hingewiesen
hat, und welches durch die Inschrift eindeutig vom Künstler als ein solches
ausgewiesen wird, ist ein gutes Beispiel dafür, welche Rolle das Selbstbildnis für
den Künstler spielen kann. Duchamp wird es damals gesehen haben.

Im neuzeitlichen Phänomen des eigenständigen Künstlerportraits steht die
Frage der Mimesis im Zentrum. Dies nicht nur, um eine künstlerische Fähigkeit
unter Beweis zu stellen, sondern auch, um eine Glaubwürdigkeit zu erreichen, die
auf den wissenschaftlichen Erkenntnissen der Zeit basiert. Den kunsttheoretischen
Traktaten Leone Battista Albertis von 1435 folgend, findet das Künstlerportrait im
antiken Mythos des Narziss seine Begründung:

„Deshalb sage ich unter Freunden, dass Narziss, der sich in eine Blume
verwandelte, folgt man den Dichtern, der Erfinder der Malerei war. Wenn schon
die Malerei die Blume aller Kunst sei, ist die Geschichte sehr passend. Was sonst
kann man Malerei nennen, als einer ähnlichen Umarmung mit der Kunst dessen,
was präsentiert wurde auf der Oberfläche der Quelle.«[2]

Das Antlitz im Spiegel der Wasseroberfläche als Wiege der Malerei! Man
könnte nun einwenden: Hoffmanns Portrait von Duchamp ist kein Selbstbildnis
im klassischen Sinne. Aber die Auffassung, dass ein nicht selbst gefertigter
Gegenstand eine künstlerische Aussage in sich tragen kann, findet sich in den
Readymades von Duchamp wieder, die er seit dieser Phase in München konzipierte.
Die Frage, inwieweit Regieanweisungen Duchamps den indifferenten Ausdruck,
ja, das Pokerface der Aufnahme hervorriefen, ist nicht überliefert. Hoffmanns

übliche Portraits der Zeit sind jedenfalls konventioneller. Das Duchamp-Portrait hat etwas Soldatisches, ja Kriegerisches. Seine Züge stellen eine emotionslose Absichtslosigkeit zur Schau. Im Rahmen damaliger Portraitfotografie, gut eine Dekade vor der Neuen Sachlichkeit, handelt es sich um eine vehemente Geste, eine Entscheidung ohne narrativen Kontext.

Dieses seltsam anmutende Portrait Duchamps zeigte Rudolf Herz im Laufe mehrerer Jahre 17 Straßenmalern in Paris. Sie fertigten in seinem Auftrag Zeichnungen nach dieser Fotografie an: mit ihren je eigenen Mitteln, ihrer je eigenen künstlerischen Handschrift, die im Französischen mit dem schönen Begriff ›la patte‹, die Pfote, umschrieben werden kann. Heraus kamen 17 Portraits, die unterschiedlicher kaum sein könnten. Die zeichnerischen Interpretationen reagieren wie die Bergnymphe Echo auf das fotografische Portrait des sich selbstbespiegelnden Narziss. Ohne eigene Formulierfähigkeit sind sie darauf verwiesen, nur die fotografische Vorgabe – verzerrt – zurückzuwerfen. Aber sie unterlaufen dabei den Anschein des sachlich nüchternen Portraits, als ob sie die im fotografischen Bildnis mitzudenkende Ablehnung der Malerei durch den portraitierten Künstler in das Gegenteil verkehren wollten.

Dass das Portrait als bloße Verdoppelung der Natur einen Mangel an Imagination, Phantasie und höherem Erkenntnisvermögen aufweist, war die Kritik der platonischen Kunstauffassung. Denn das Ziel ist nicht nur, etwas dem Portraitierten Ähnliches zu schaffen, sondern das wahre Bild, ähnlicher als bloß das der äußeren Physiognomie des Dargestellten, auszudrücken.

Duchamps Portrait ist somit durchaus als Memorandum zu verstehen, dessen fehlender Kontext, Inschriften, Kleidung, Ort, Mimik, Bewegung und Stimmung, auf die künstlerische Haltung schließen lassen soll. Sich selbst durch ein Bildnis von sich zu erklären, impliziert nicht zuletzt eine Reflexion seines Inneren, symbolisch durch die Spiegelung und somit der äußeren Erscheinungsform. Die Originalität des Narziss-Mythos für eine »ursprüngliche« Bestimmung der Portraitmalerei wiederholt sich in dem immer wieder behaupteten Wechselverhältnis der Genese der Portraitmalerei mit der Entdeckung der Individualität.[3]

Die Verknüpfung dieser beiden Ausgangspunkte in einem gemeinsamen Ursprungsmythos ist zwar selbst spekulativ, denn sie bindet die Selbstbetrachtung notwendig an die Selbsterkenntnis. Wenn nun aber durch die Expressivität und

Handschriftlichkeit der Moderne alle Malerei ein Selbstbildnis der Innerlichkeit ist, dann folgte daraus für Duchamp, dass man sich wieder der Außenwelt zuwenden muss, wenn man sich von der Bespiegelung eben dieser Innerlichkeit abgrenzen will. Sich also der Umgebung wieder zuzuwenden, die Aufmerksamkeit wieder auf das Soziale zu lenken, dem in der Individuation dem Subjekt Gegenüberstehenden, das wäre die »Wiederversöhnung der Kunst mit dem Volk«, wie es sich Apollinaire von Duchamps ästhetischer Vorbehaltslosigkeit versprach.

Die Arbeit von Herz setzt sich kritisch mit der dekonstruktiven Absage Duchamps an die Malerei auseinander, indem sie die Dekonstruktion auf ihren Ursprung zurückführt. Die Frage, die die 17 Portraits der Straßenmaler stellen, könnte lauten: Wie kann man dem Drang nachgeben, künstlerisch tätig sein zu wollen, wenn man zugleich beschließt, damit aufzuhören? Ein neuer Begriff muss her. Eine Transformation. Eine neue Sichtweise auf die Dinge, die man bislang tat, die für einen selbst unbefriedigende Ergebnisse gezeigt haben. Schwer zu sagen, ob es Duchamp nur auf die Bestätigung von außen oder um eine intrinsische Motivation ankam, die er in München suchte. Zumindest spricht die Tatsache, dass er für diese Transformation die Distanz zu Paris suchte, dafür, dass es ihm eher um Letzteres ging, dass er sich nicht beeinflussen lassen wollte von negativer wie positiver Aufmerksamkeit der Kritiker oder Künstlerkollegen. Wie auch immer … Vielleicht war es auch einfach nur der Schmerz einer unerfüllten Liebe, der ihn in die Ferne trieb.

---

1) Zitiert nach: Daniels, Dieter: Duchamp und die Anderen. Der Modellfall einer künstlerischen Wirkungsgeschichte in der Moderne. Köln 1992, S. 48.

2) Alberti, Leon Battista: La Pittura. Übers. Lodovico Domenichi, Venedig 1547, Sala Bolognese 1988, S.19.

3) Vgl. Boehm, Gottfried: Bildnis und Individuum. Über den Ursprung der Portraitmalerei in der italienischen Renaissance, München 1985.

Tafelteil / Plates

HOIE

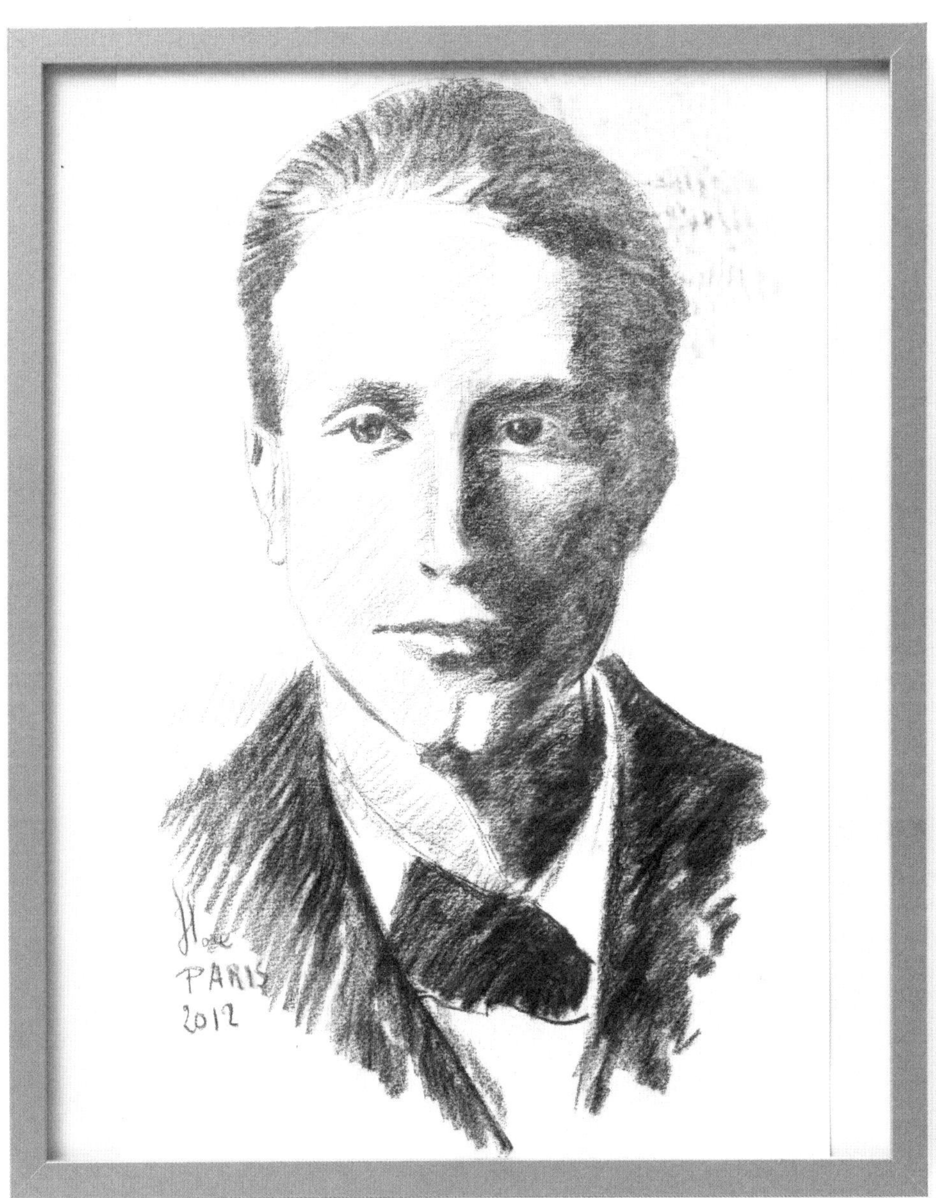
PARIS
2012

LINDA GALIC

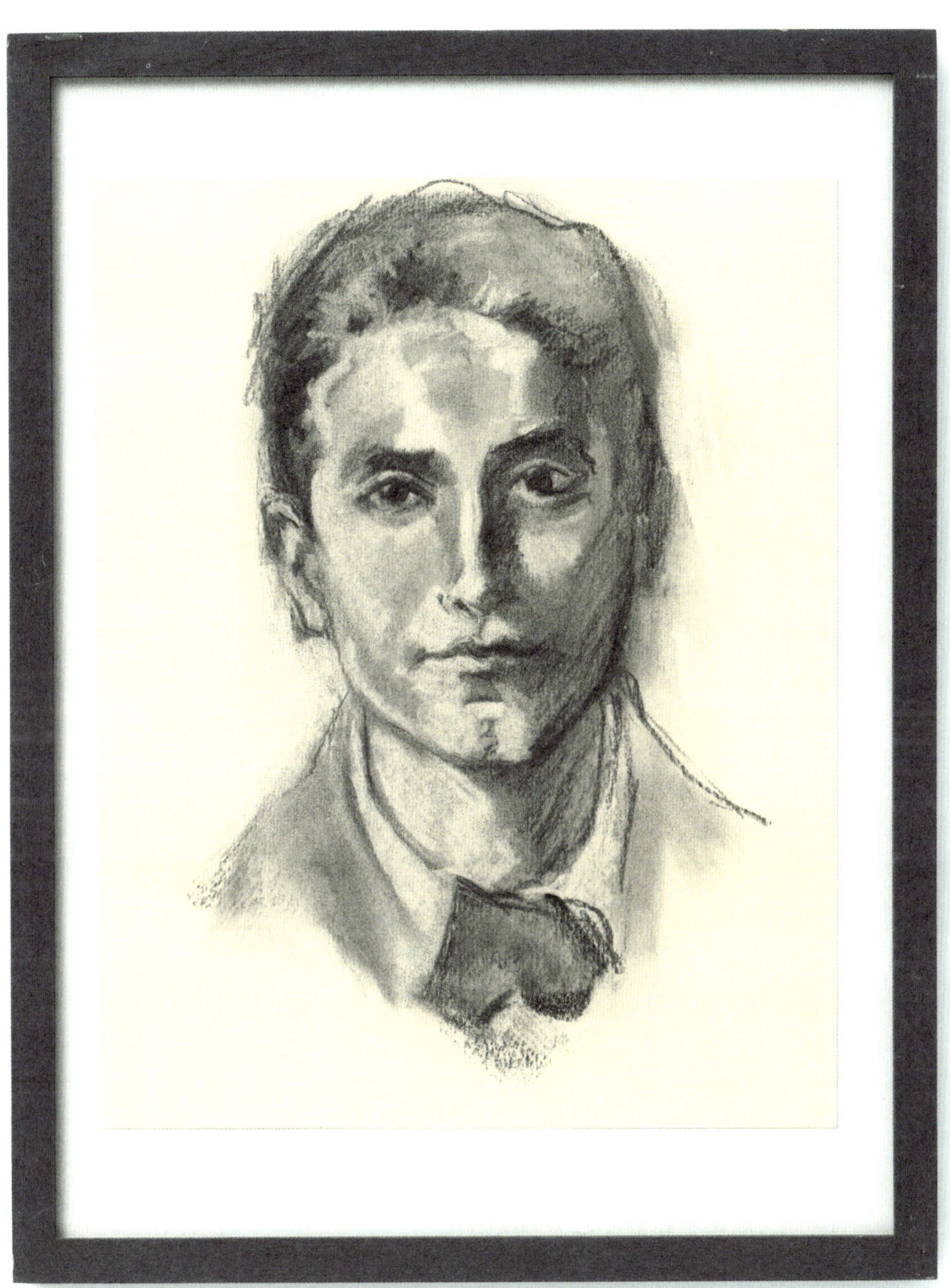

AMERY

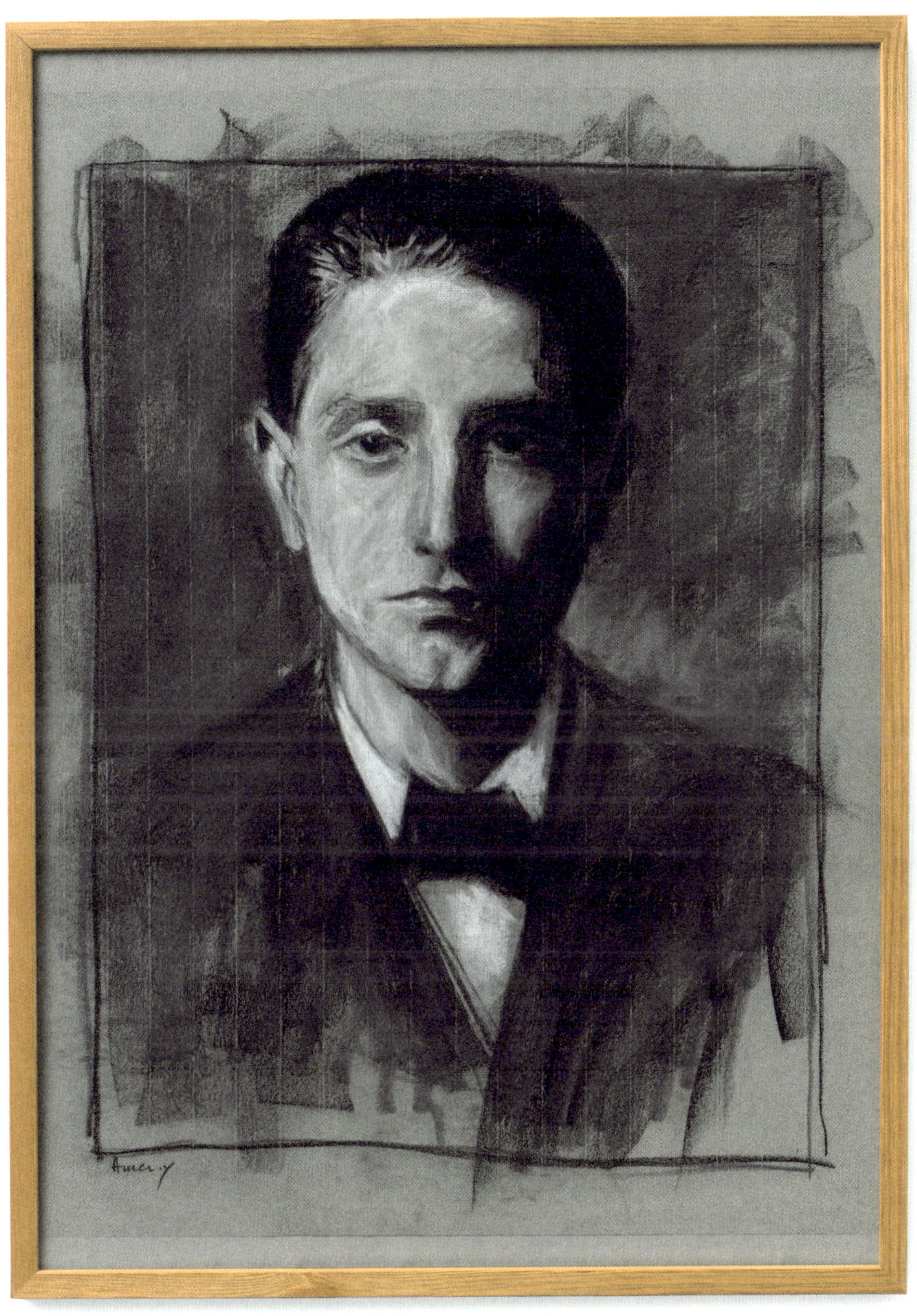

GALINA KONOPITSKAYA

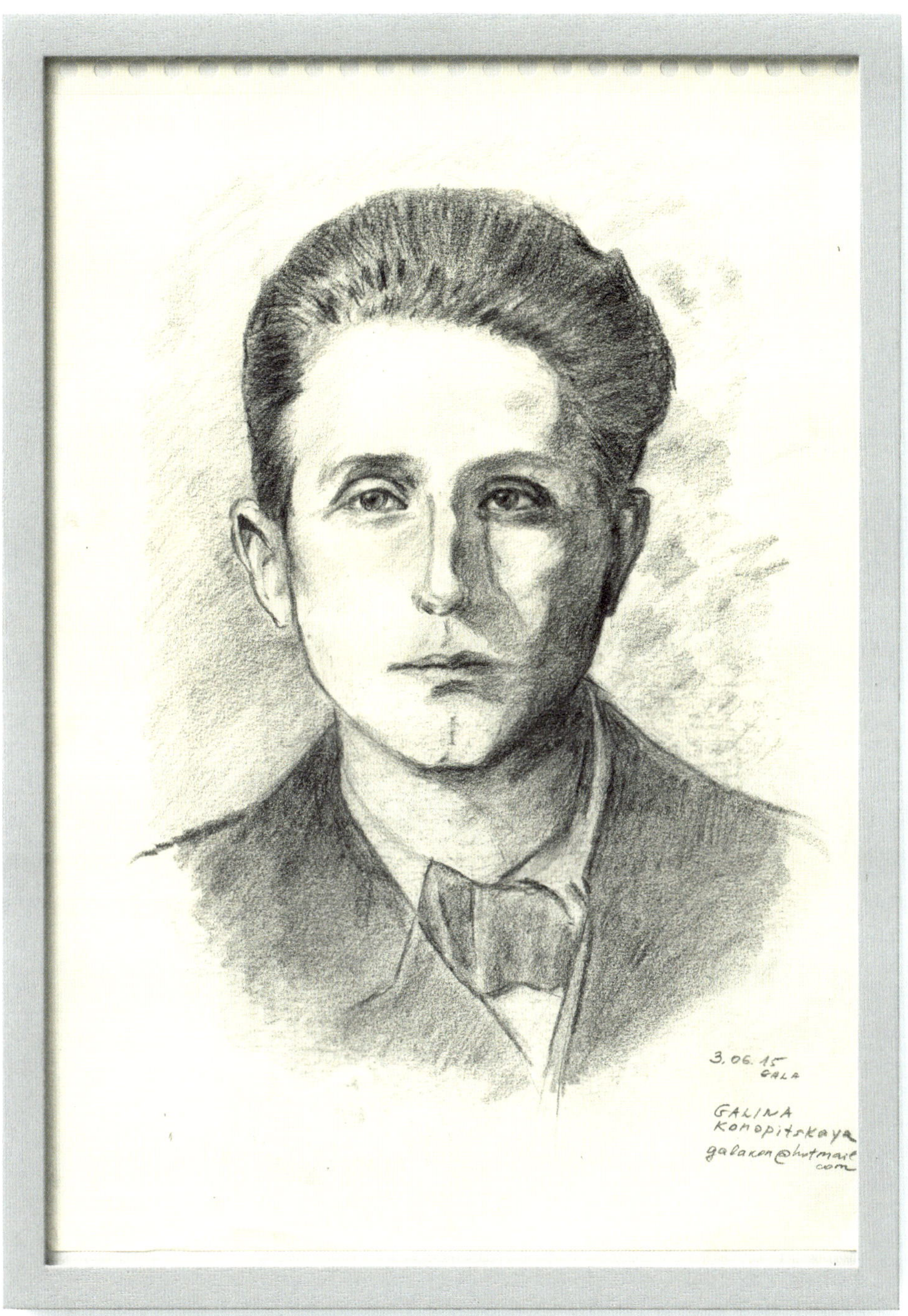

3.06.15
GALA
GALINA
Konopitskaya
galakon@hotmail.com

O. PIREZ PERTUS

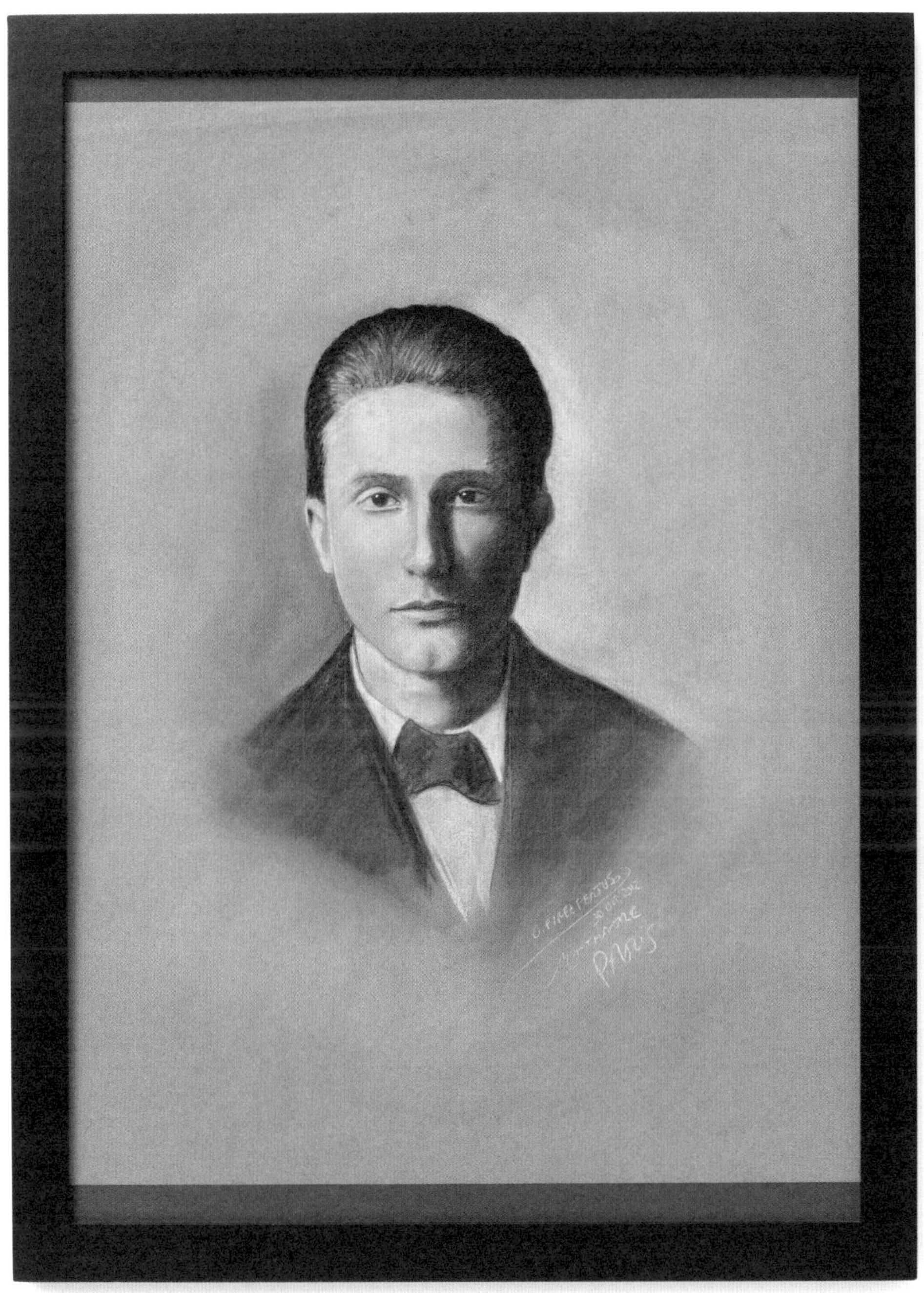

BONNO

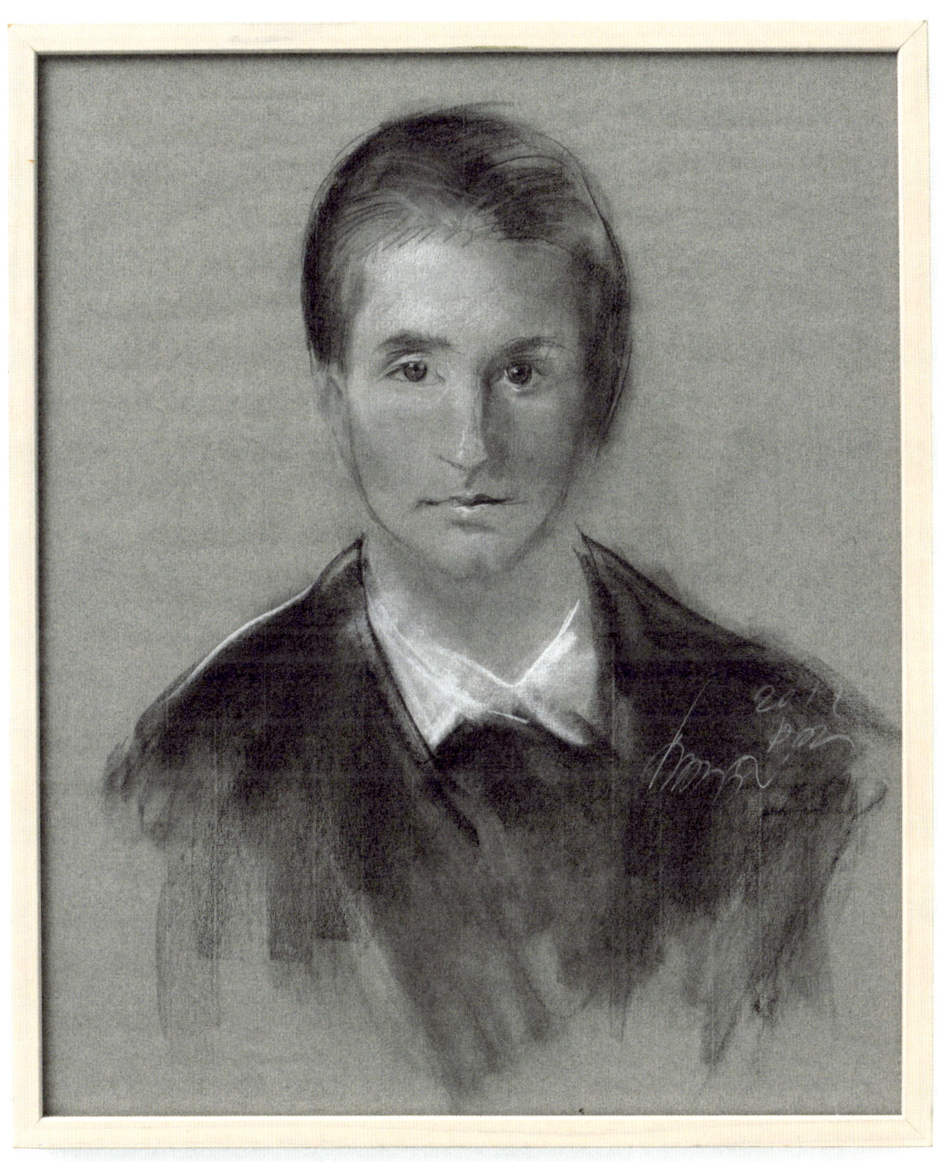

STÉPHANE PLOUVIEZ

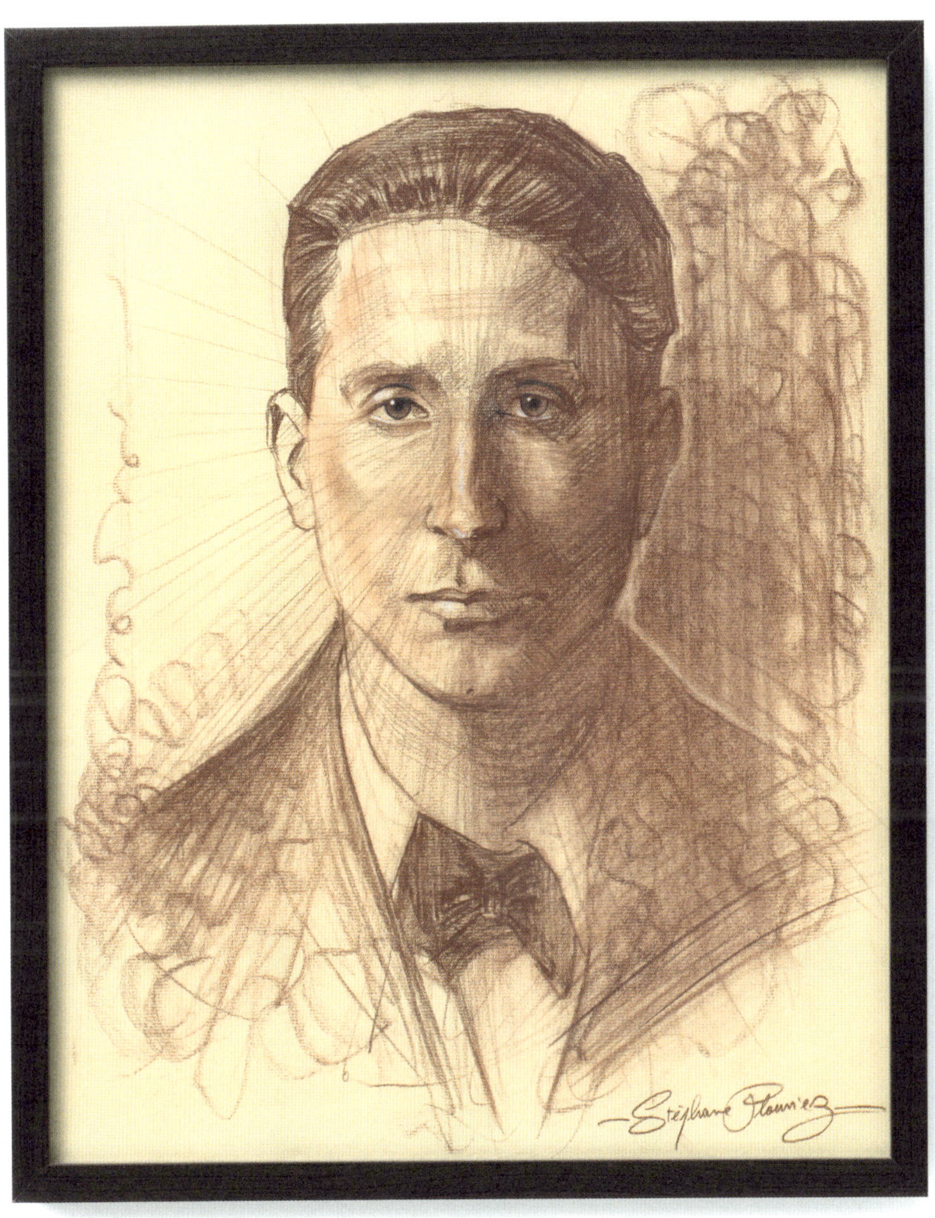

MOHAI

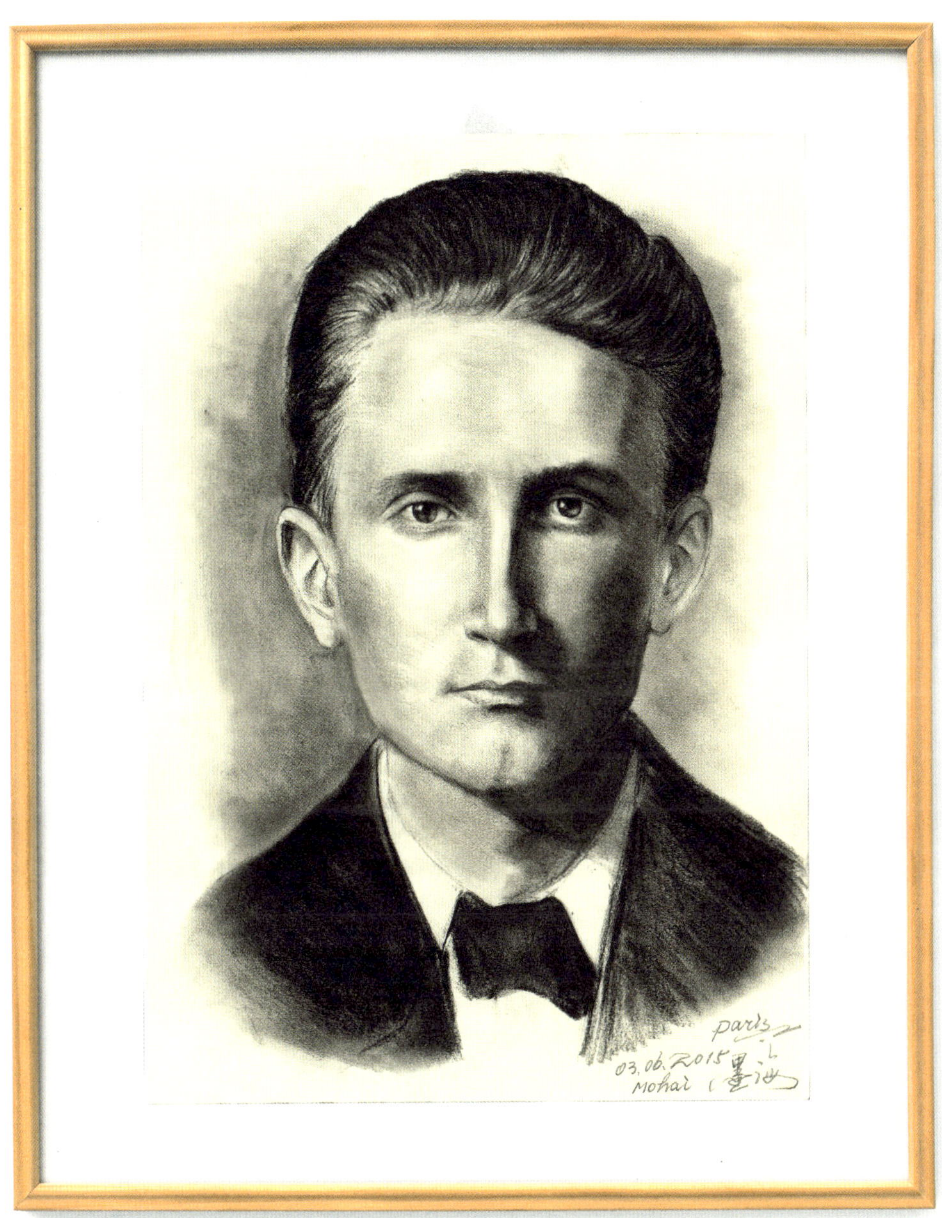

paris
03. 06. 2015 墨海
Mohai

EDUARD

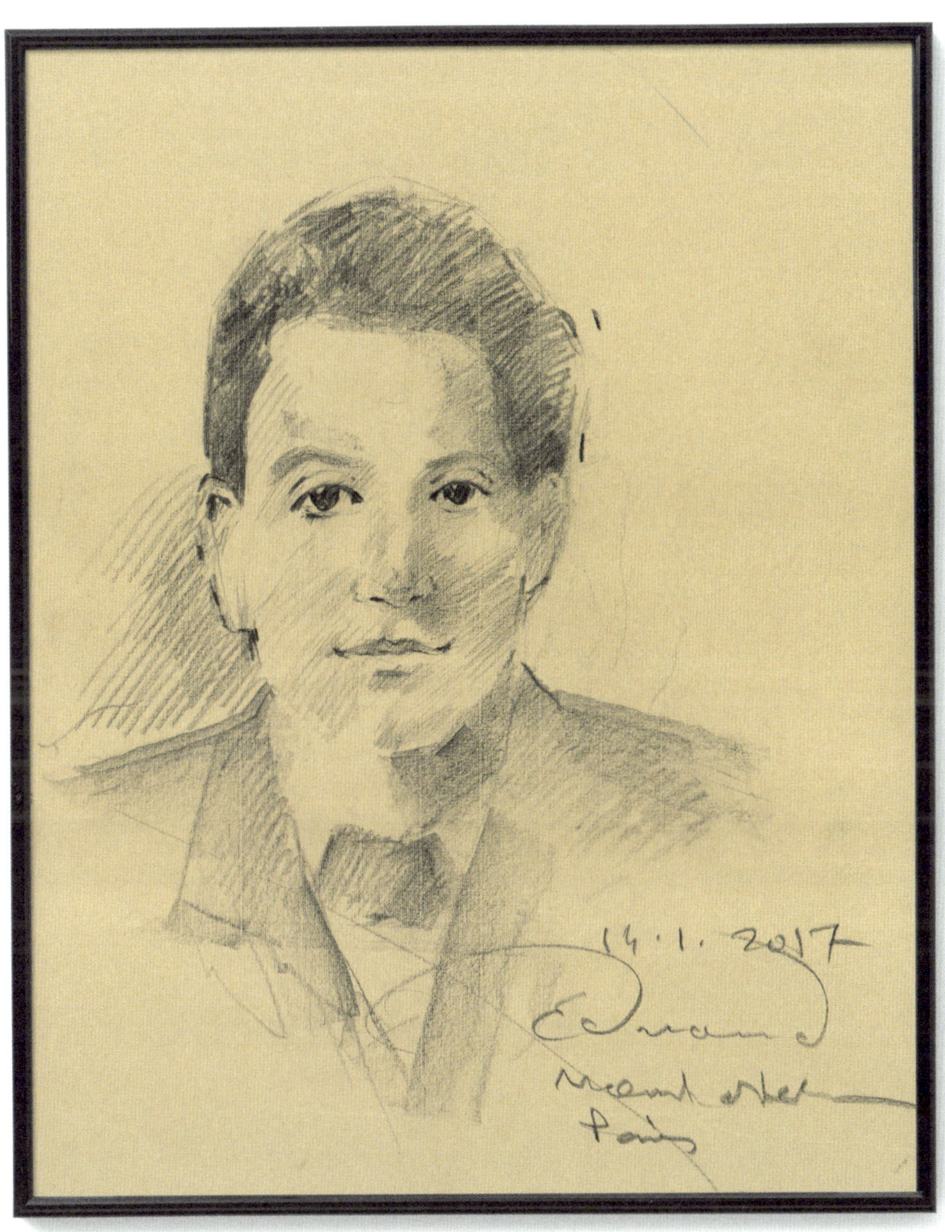

JAFFAR

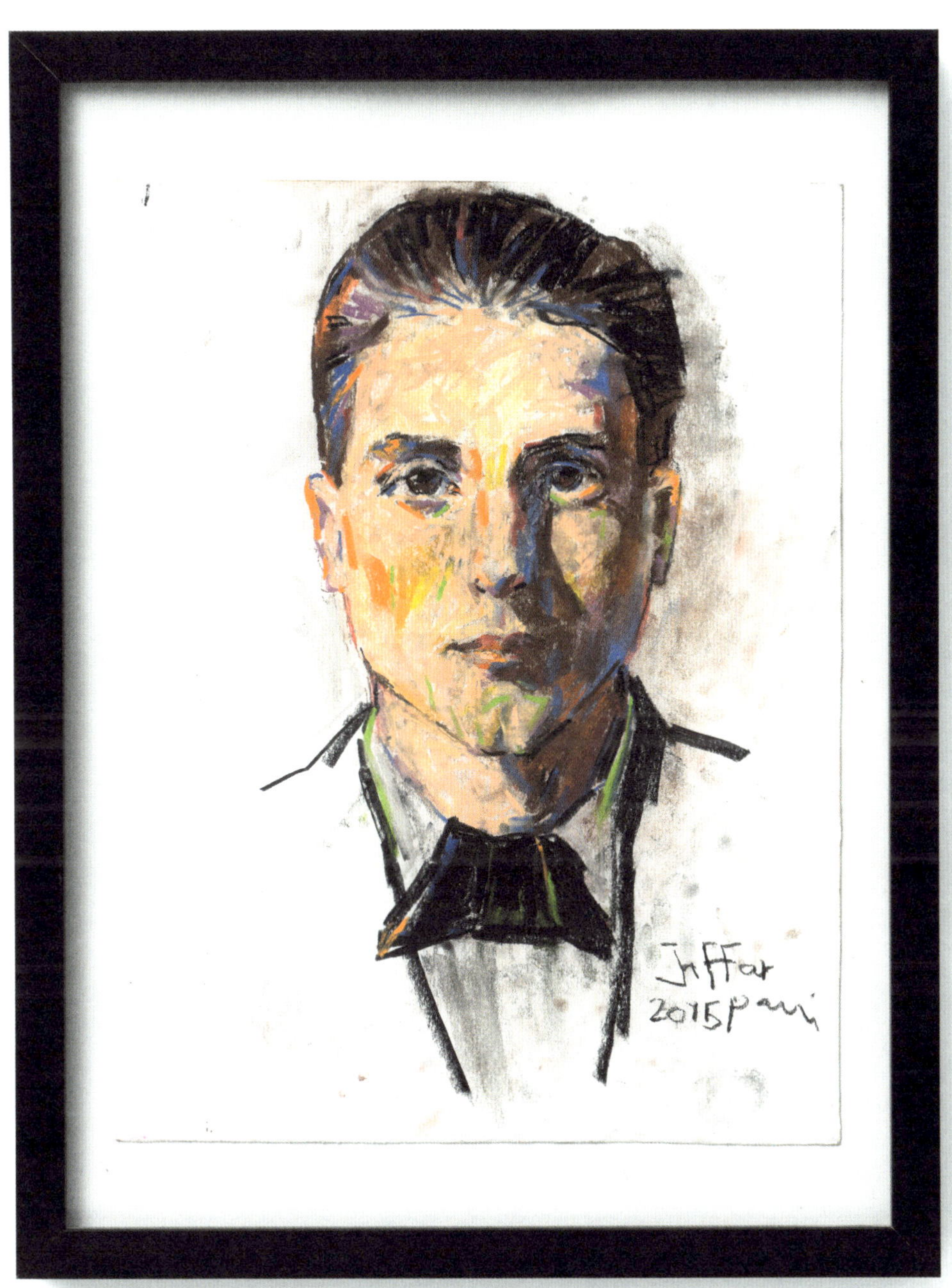

Jaffar
2015 Paris

SUILIC

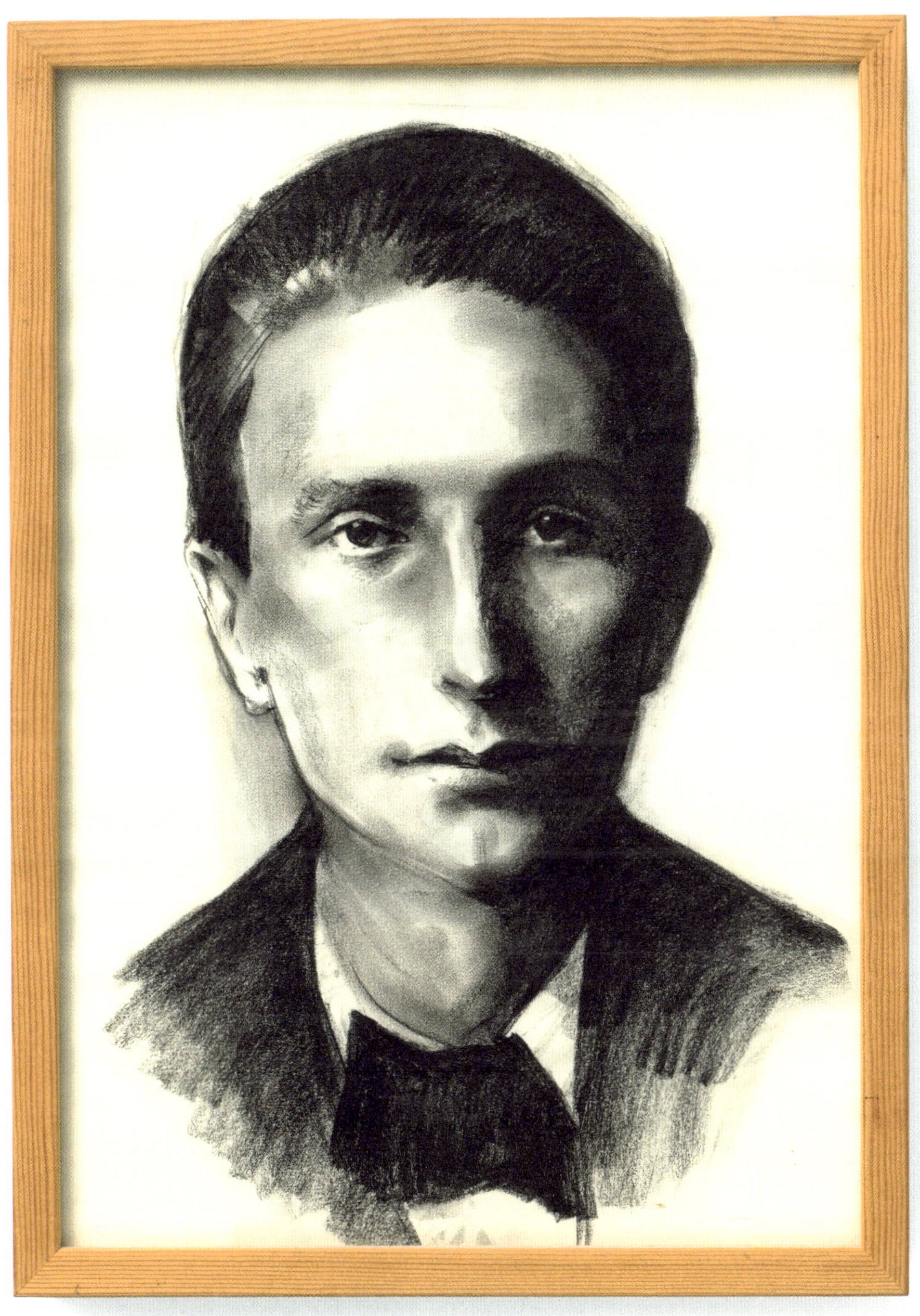

LES SATAN

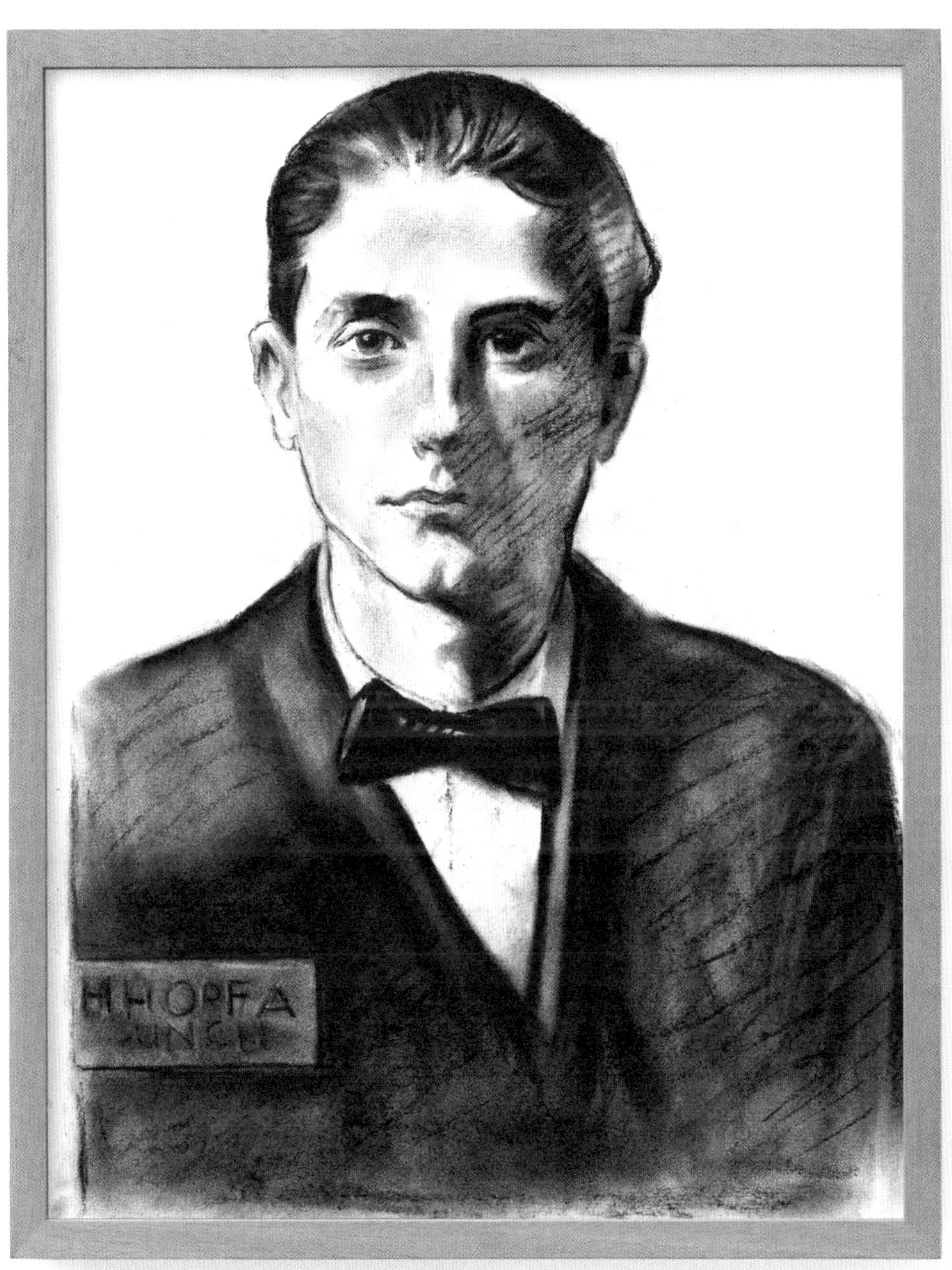
H. HOPFA
MÜNCHEN

COPPERFIELD

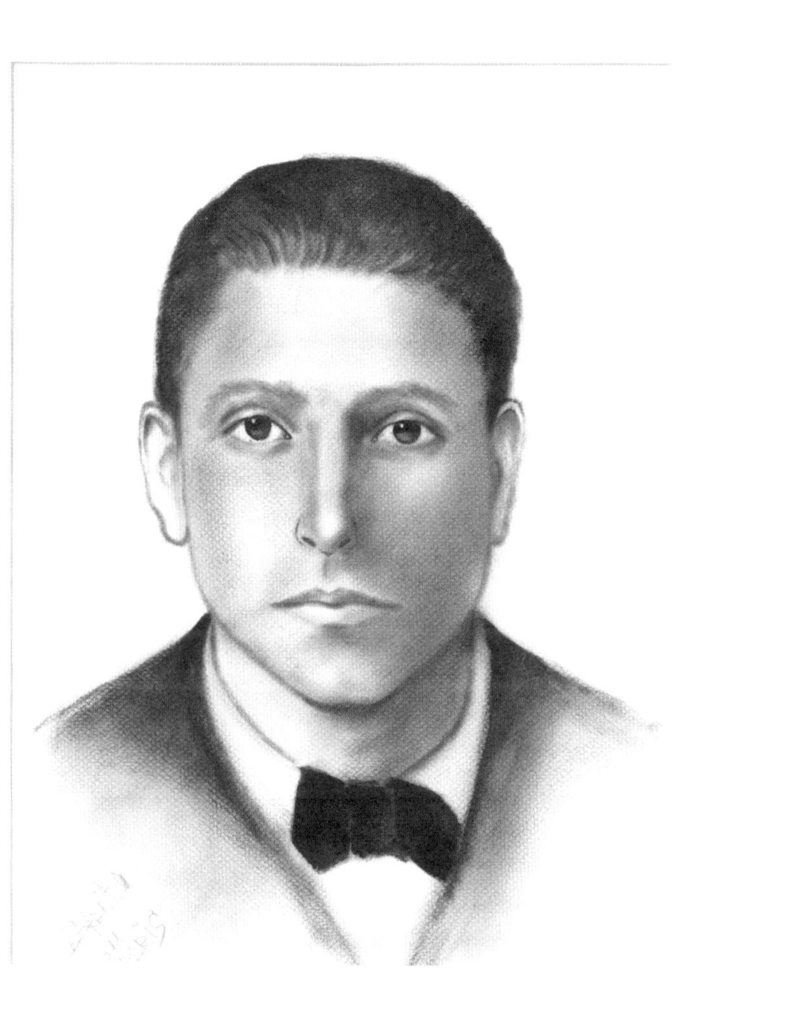

MAJID

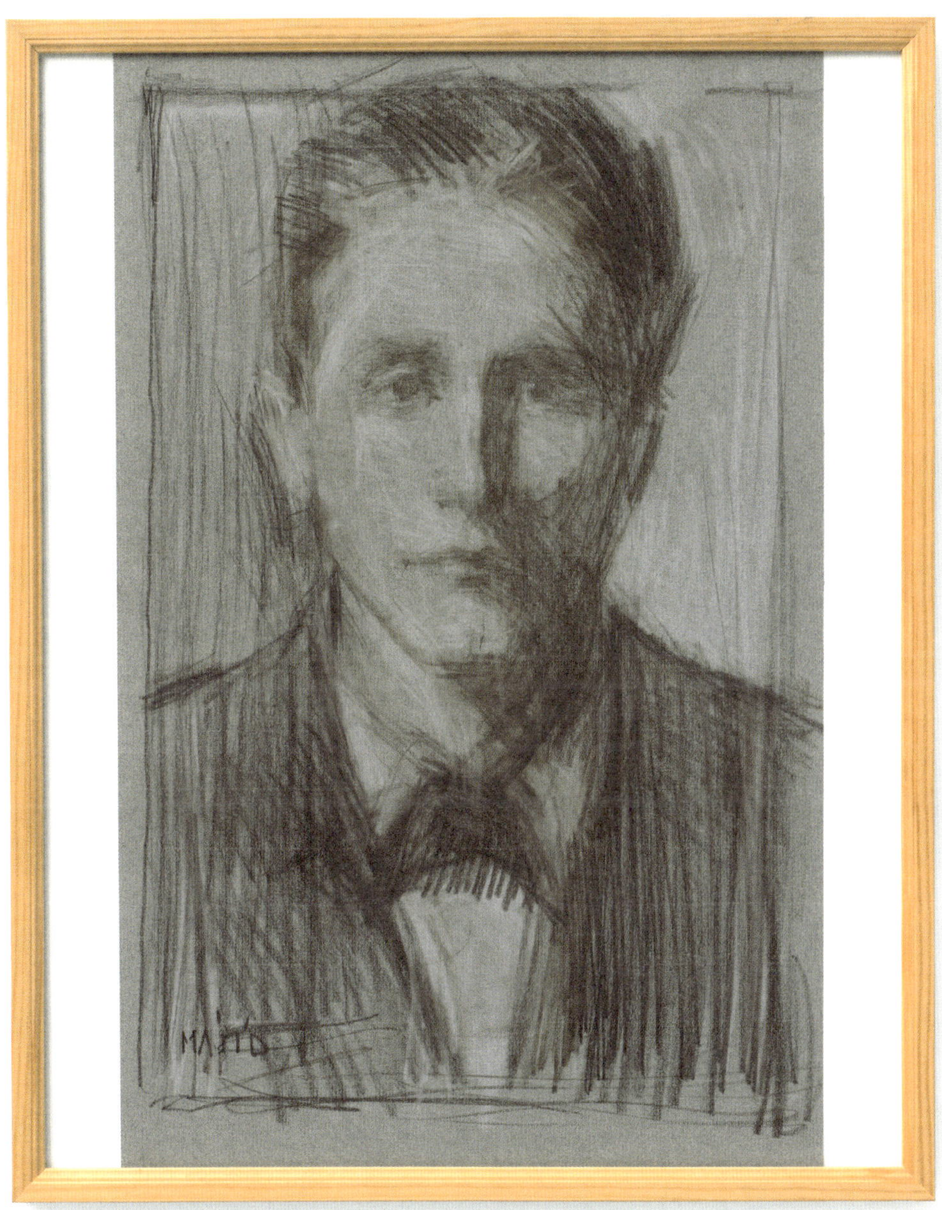

IDK

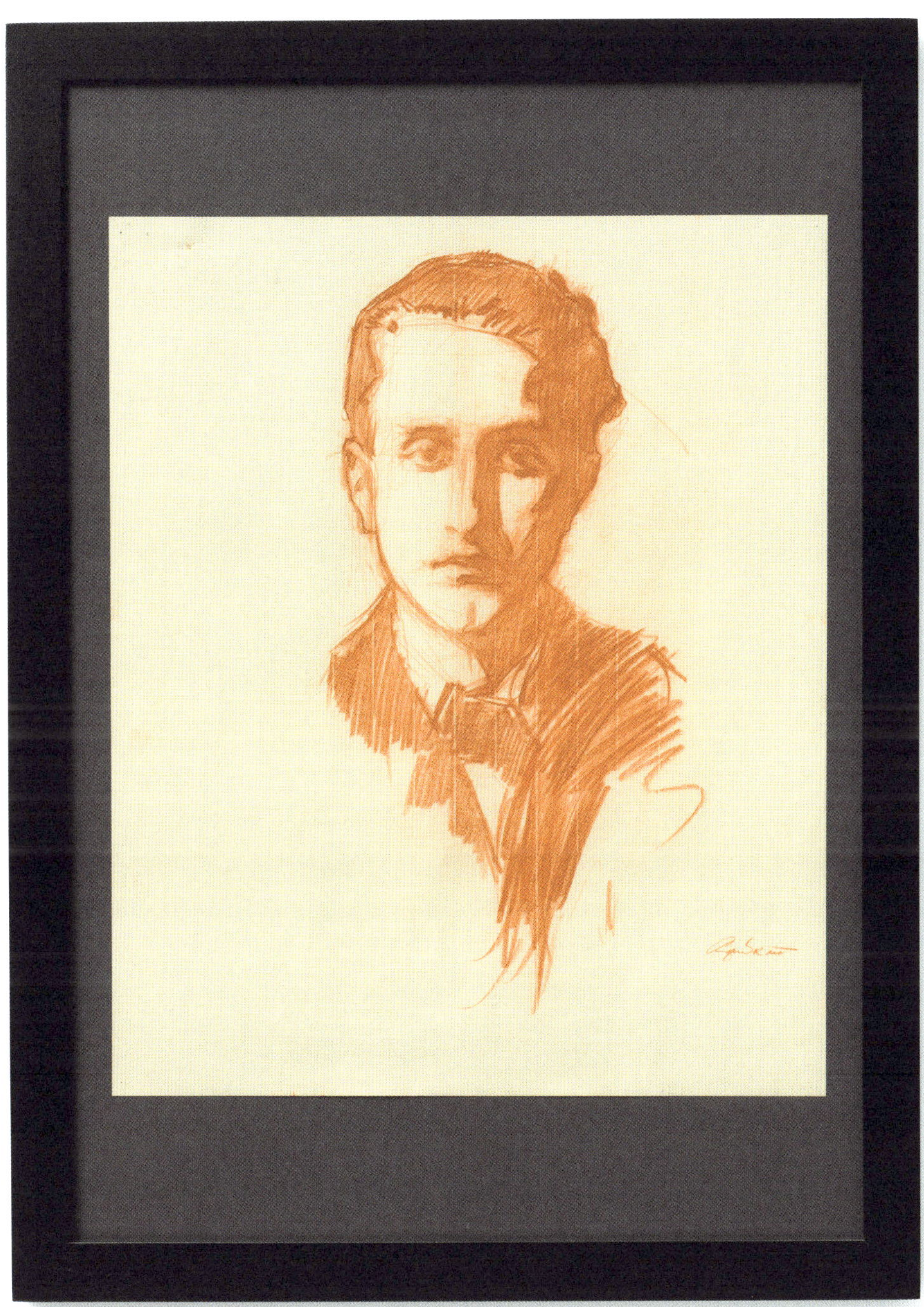

DANY JIM

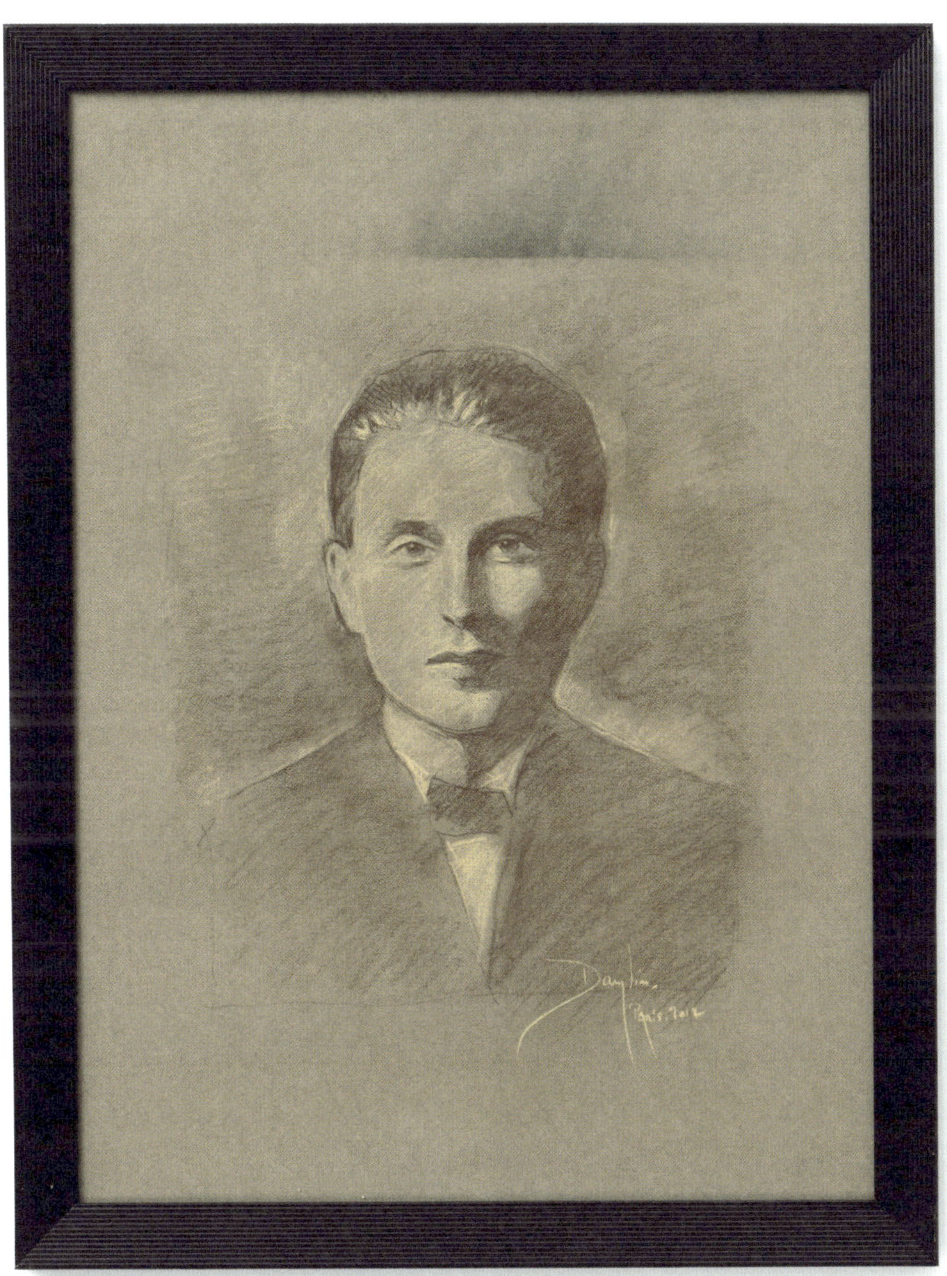

IDK

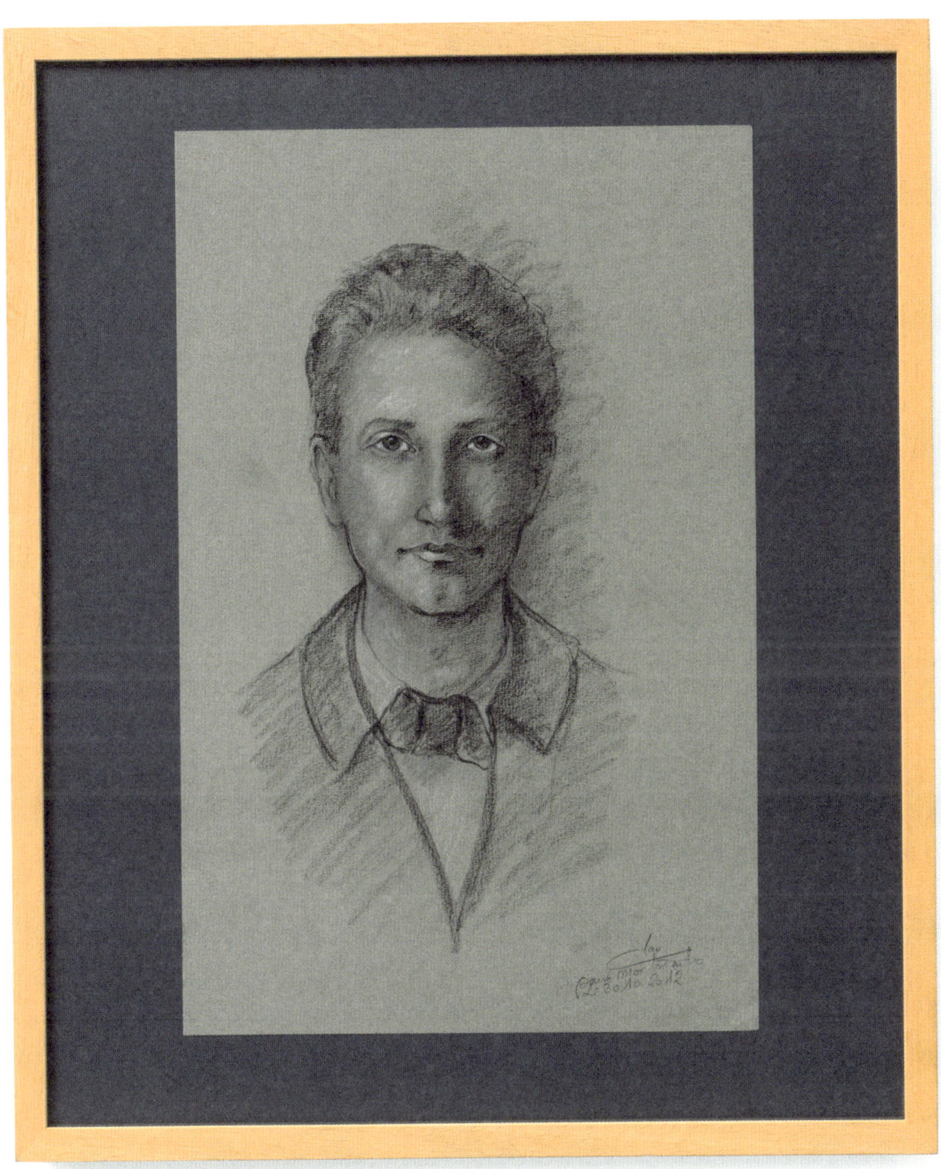

PHILIPP NORMAN JOHN / MARIE-JOSÉ SONDEIJKER

Paris-Munich-Paris

Marcel Duchamp's work has inspired Rudolf Herz on many occasions. Over the years he has sought to engage with this work and dared to experiment aesthetically: provocative spatial installations, a sculptural setting in public spaces, lettering made of white smoke in the sky. He has undertaken historical-critical research in order to open up a new approach. He is not alone in this; artists such as Serge Stauffer and Stefan Banz have also explored Duchamp's paths.

The impulse came from a little-known portrait photograph of Duchamp that Herz came across during his art studies. It was taken in the summer of 1912, when the 25-year-old Duchamp spent three months in Munich. In a first artistic venture with this portrait, Herz produced large-format screen prints and contrasted them in the chessboard-like room installation ›Zugzwang‹ (Kunstverein Ruhr, Essen 1996, The Jewish Museum, New York City 2002 and other locations) with screen prints in the same size of a portrait of Adolf Hitler. The installation creates a network of relationships that is not easily resolved and puts our understanding of the image to the test. For Herz, the fact that both portraits are by Hitler's later ›court photographer‹ Hoffmann is little more than coincidence.

Throughout his life, Duchamp tried to cover up the traces of his stay in Munich, even though these months probably represent the most momentous period of his artistic biography. In the detective-style project ›Marcel Duchamp. Le Mystère de Munich‹ (Architekturmuseum der TU München 2012), Rudolf Herz illuminated the background in detail. The Munich flat in which Duchamp lived as a subtenant in 1912 – for Herz the cradle of conceptual art – took centre stage.

A decisive factor in Duchamp's time in Munich was the specific experience of modern technology, which was to radically change his understanding of art and lead to his departure from painting. It also freed him from the endeavour to create a personal style, which he called »la patte« – paw, paw – using a slightly polemical French term. Following this new approach came the readymades, and soon afterwards he tackled his masterpiece ›The Large Glass‹. According to Rudolf Herz's thesis, Duchamp's portrait already anticipated this development.

Herz responded to Duchamp's rejection of »la patte«, the artistic signature, with an initiative in the opposite direction. He commissioned 17 Parisian street artists to make copies of the Munich portrait. He gave them a completely free hand and was curious to see how the interpretations would turn out. Indeed, the stylistic spectrum of the drawings and the diversity of the personality profiles sketched are surprising.

We are delighted to be able to present the results of the Parisian artists under the title ›Marcel Duchamp. La Patte‹, and to exhibit the complete series of drawings for the first time. This publication reproduces the series of portraits, accompanied by three texts that analyse various aspects of the project and its genesis.

RUDOLF HERZ

Marcel Duchamp. La Patte

In the course of my research on Marcel Duchamp I more often travelled to Paris, where I also began to visit the street painters on Montmartre. At one point I asked them to make copies of the portrait of Marcel Duchamp taken by the photographer Heinrich Hoffmann during his stay in Munich in 1912. 17 drawings were created in this way, with distinctly different styles. I have compiled them under the title ›Marcel Duchamp. La Patte‹.

The Parisian street artists wanted to know exactly whose picture I was showing them. Not all were familiar with Duchamp. When I later showed the drawings to friends and colleagues, the spontaneous reaction was a comparative judgement: this portrait is much more like Duchamp than that one, and that one, that's funny! Beyond questions of quality, I find it interesting what contrasting perceptions and personality profiles the drawings create and what character and social conjectures they evoke. There is the androgynous schoolboy, the cowboy, the subtle intellectual, the Mexican drug baron or the absinthe consumer in delirium. It is precisely this sum of interpretative possibilities that I find remarkable.

Ever since I saw Duchamp's portrait for the first time, it has stayed with me. It has spurred me on to pursue very different projects. ›Marcel Duchamp. La Patte‹ ironically revolves around the phenomenon of artistic drawing style. At the time when Duchamp had himself photographed by Hoffmann, he was faced with the question of how he should use this same style in his art in the future. My thesis is that his imminent departure from it is already reflected in the conception of this portrait photograph. So this shot points to the development to come.

I asked myself: why, when Guillaume Apollinaire asked him for a portrait for his Cubism book in the summer of 1912, did Duchamp have himself photographed

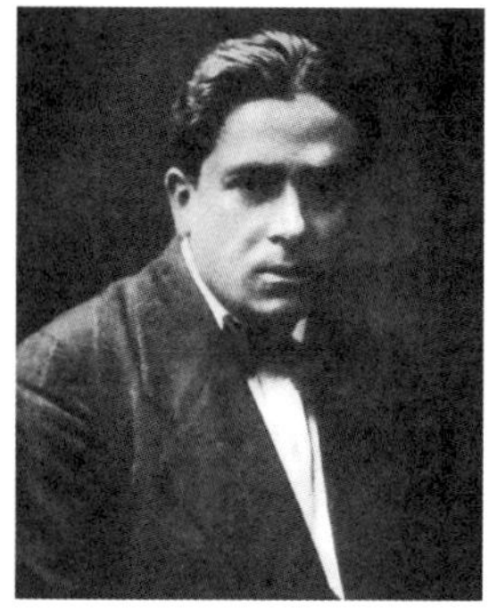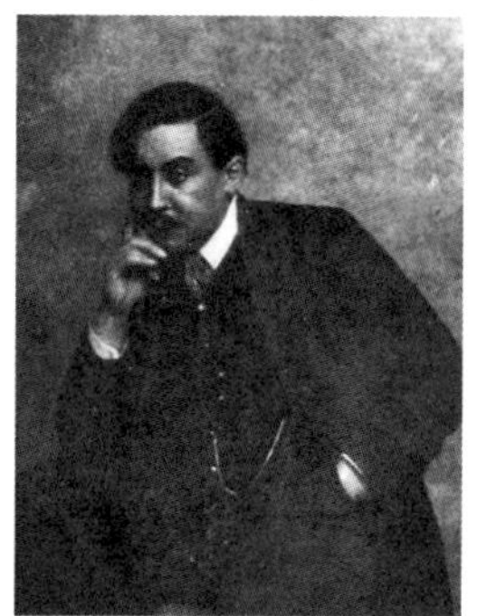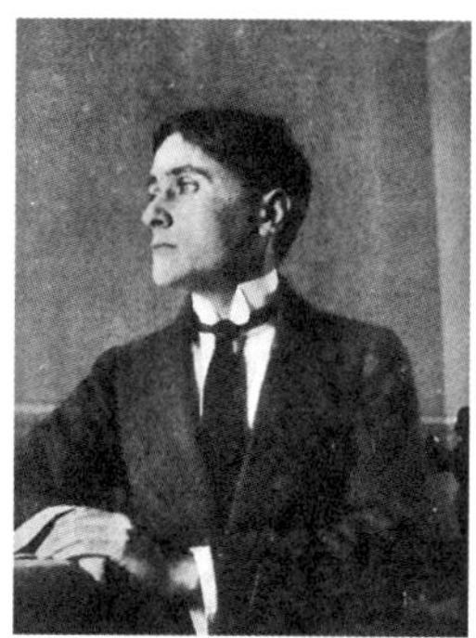

Francis Picabia, Albert Gleizes, Jean Metzinger, in: Guillaume Apollinaire: Méditations Esthétiques. Les Peintres Cubistes, Paris 1913

in this sterile manner? He looks bored, with the frozen face of a statue or porcelain doll, not seeking intense eye contact. He adopts the attitude of indifference that he was later to propagate as an artistic stance.

The portrait is quite atypical for the studio photography that was common at the time, as well as for portraits of artists at the time. You can see this when you compare it with the very individual portraits of fellow artists Francis Picabia, Albert Gleizes and Jean Metzinger in Apollinaire's book, all of whom endeavour to use painterly values and manipulations that can be classified as contemporary art photography. Duchamp clearly wanted to distance himself from this. The result of Hoffmann's portrait session is reminiscent of administrative passport and police photographs, which know no psychological empathy and are unconcerned with emotion and individual expression: an anatomical data sheet that treats the person as a mere object. This cool approach, this technical-machine concept, is an artistic achievement, a method that Duchamp owes to his stay in Munich.

Specifically, it was his visual experiences at the Deutsches Museum and at an industrial trade fair that probably led him to this approach. Last but not least, the close contact with his young landlords at Barer Strasse 65 will have played a role: a seamstress and an experienced engineer at the Maffei locomotive factory, who had previously headed the technical drawing department at Oldenbourg Verlag. The 12-square-metre room in this flat overlooking Barer Strasse, which Duchamp found offered in a newspaper advertisement, became the centre of

64

his new insights and his work during his three-month stay in Munich. This room, I claim, is the cradle of conceptual art! Together with the architect Peter Ottmann, I transformed the flat into a large sculpture on a scale of 1:1, tilted it 90 degrees and placed it in front of the Alte Pinakothek.

Duchamp's new approach was soon reflected in the development of the readymades and the concept of the ›Large Glass‹. Looking back, he explained that it was not even the depiction of movement in the spectacular work ›Nude Descending a Staircase‹ that »opened a window to something else« for him, but rather technical depictions and technical drawings. His polemic against »retinal painting«, the impression made by the eye, went hand in hand with his polemic against »artistic style«. He said to his biographer Calvin Tomkins in 1965: »The point was to forget my hand.« And elsewhere: »There is an old expression in French: ›la patte‹, which describes an artist's brushstroke, his personal style, his ›paw‹. I wanted to get away from ›la patte‹ and from all this retinal painting … from 1912 I decided to stop being a painter in the professional sense.«

Duchamp's portrait is without a »paw«, reduced to the utmost. It contains a minimum of information about the person, it is the radical negation of a personal

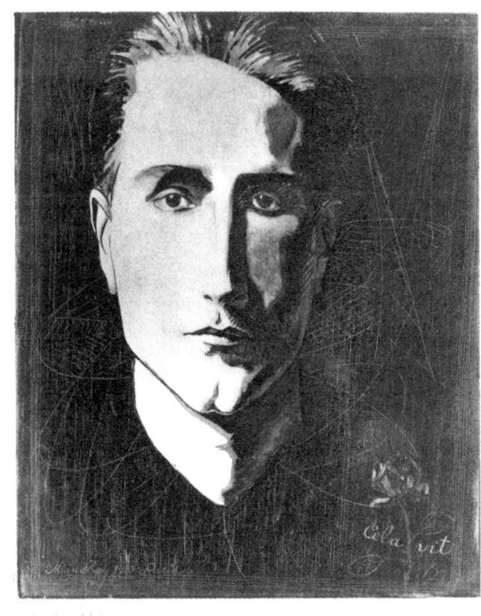

Man Ray: Cela vit, 1923

style. Duchamp thus applied his new concept to his own portrait as early as 1912. It is something like an attempt at a photographic zero point, liberated from body language and aesthetic ingredients. It can be assumed that the creative decision lay solely with Duchamp, and that Hoffmann only had to operate the camera. One could also speak in this respect of Duchamp's self-portrait.

In ›Marcel Duchamp. La Patte‹, the Parisian street artists attack Duchamp, as it were, and unmistakably impose their »paw« on his dry portrait. My project counteracts Duchamp's original approach, and as a result the artists not only bring their own »paw« to bear, but also individualise Duchamp in a variety of ways. And the sum of their portraits opens up an experimental role play full of contrasts. And here it is not a case of »either or«, »but both«. One could also see stills from a morphologically conceived film in the individual drawings and imagine a cinematic spectacle of changing identities.

The Paris drawings are not alone. As early as 1923, Man Ray used Hoffmann's photograph of Duchamp as the basis for the aquatint etching ›Cela Vit‹. He gave Duchamp a suggestively dramatic appearance; the young man could be an actor or a film star. Man Ray also photographed Duchamp's self-created androgynous alter ego ›Rrose Sélavy‹, a pseudonym that until then had only served him as a signature. Duchamp fashioned himself as an older, melancholic-looking woman. He played with the traditional distribution of roles and the heteronomous relationship between the sexes.

Duchamp never let go of the transformation of his own self. He developed an artistic strategy from this, and even anticipated his own ageing when he staged himself as an aged artist-philosopher with the photograph ›at the age of 85‹ in New York in 1945. He was just 58 years old at the time. He knew exactly how to manipulate his face through make-up and photography in order to achieve the convincing effect of a fictional image.

Duchamp did not want to define himself as a person or his artistic conception. He refused any identity that could restrict him. He favoured experimentation and did not want to create a style. He still provokes us with this today – it is part of the logic of his idea of artistic freedom.

My great thanks go to the street painters of Paris.

ANTJE VON GRAEVENITZ

Marcel Duchamp's ›Portrait-Object‹, revived

How tempting it is to be drawn by a Parisian street artist! You would love to know how he perceives and depicts you. Will his portrait be similar to how I know myself, or completely different? Does it focus on an unknown or hidden character trait that only this artist can »bring out«?

Long before there were photo portraits, drawn reproductions of a face were commonplace. Those who knew how to draw true to life were usually successful. A model hoped to finally see what they looked like, possibly differently than in the mirror. They also wished to be able to recognise how others (as a pars pro toto for everyone) would perceive them, because an interpretation flowed quite naturally into the lines via the drawing hand. In addition, the fact that that moment in life could survive through the drawing was welcome: young and perhaps beautiful, or expressive and possibly wise. People wanted to be surprised: what identity did one's own self have in it? People patiently sat in front of the artist as a model – whether at home, in the studio or on the street – and waited for the result. For a long time this artistic procedure was not a matter of course. It only became common practice at least at the end of the Middle Ages, when the ›I‹ finally found its way into the picture. When drawn, it was soon used for a collection, as a pledge for a contract, as a profile or even as an advertisement for a marriage contract, if the actual bride still lived far away and her facial image was already supposed to trigger feelings in the potential groom. So a picture of the face became an important ›thing‹. It's hard to imagine, in our age of the selfie, what a revolution this was.

The history of portrait photography is probably equally astonishing today, because a few years after the invention (1826) of photographic technology, from 1839 onwards it was initially a privilege of the wealthy to have themselves photographed in long sessions in front of the camera. This also became a ›thing‹: it was used as a ‚carte de visite' for social attention, and against oblivion. The models concerned probably looked at the photographed result in amazement: mostly as a serious and fixed-looking face, which they thought captured real, true life in the picture much more realistically than any drawing. The idea that a photographer would also contribute his or her interpretation of the model remained undiscussed for a long time. It was believed that a photograph accurately reflected reality. It would correspond to an exact identity of the face, at least that is what doctors assumed about photographed hysterics, police officers about photos of alleged and convicted criminals, customs officials about passport photos of travellers, and ethnologists about serial photographs of (colonised) non-Europeans for the purpose of supposed scientific research. They all believed that their photo collections of direct facial images always materialised the realities of the people concerned.

In Belgium the intention was to introduce such objective facial photographs for the homeless, vagabonds, beggars and criminal suspects as early as 1870, and in France only after Alphonse Bertillon proposed the ›photographie signalétique‹ for the official recording of identities in 1882. However, he had to admit that the needs ultimately could not be met because identity is only created through differences in appearance, as Hans Belting explains in his book ›Faces. Eine Geschichte des Gesichtes‹ (2013). The more petrified their gaze appeared to the camera, the more mask-like the front appeared, the more clearly the base of the ears could be seen, the more object-like a person appeared in the facial image. Object-like – and therefore like an object to be had and handled – thus appeared the identity of each person, entirely confined in the tight frame of the facial photograph.

Here, object-like is both a keyword and a hypothesis. After all, why would Marcel Duchamp of all people allow himself to be photographed by the photographer Heinrich Hoffmann in 1912 during his stay in Munich for a book by Guillaume Apollinaire in the passport photo style with a petrified facial expression, even though he depicted movement with his picture ›Nude Descending the Stairs‹ in 1912, he who seemed to have had enough of all the reclining or seated nudes of the past? So why did Duchamp not want to bring any expression into his portrait as a sign of at least inner movement? Why did he want to avoid any psychological identity and only establish a formal identity? After all, he is looking at us with small, somewhat uneven eyes in a long face with a corresponding nose and dimples in the chin. His face »gives nothing more away«. So far at least, it resembles no other. But the rigid frontal view of the face »speaks volumes«: police photographs were only common in France for a little over 20 years and thus probably still had some »topicality« as a stylistic category. Did Duchamp want to resemble hysterics, criminals, travellers or non-Europeans? Did he, who declared until the end of his life that he was completely »indifferent« to the intention of his readymades (for example the ›Bottle Dryer‹, ›Urinoir‹ and ›Hat Rack‹), want to make use of this indifference in his portrait photo from 1912? It became his central concern, his most important theoretical goal.

Was he not interested in his likeness? Did he not want to create a photo, but a ›photo-thing‹? One that a photographer could simply produce according to banal official rules? After all, he later showed himself in the photo profile of a criminal (1923 as ›Wanted‹) or in 1921 as the lady ›Rrose Sélavy‹ on the perfume bottle ›Belle Haleine‹ and thus made it clear that he was not interested in any identity of Marcel Duchamp, but rather in a fictitious double identity that swept the ground from under his own feet. Photographed reality: did it even exist? If there were other photographs of Duchamp, for example playing chess or with friends, then they were not formally (co-)staged by him. In other words, this argument leads to the assumption that objectivity and indifference were given to the photographer Hoffmann as Duchamp's intention.

Rudolf Herz also comes to all these considerations. Nevertheless, he was not satisfied with Duchamp's verdict – as it can certainly be described. In the years from 2012 to 2017 (after an interval of one hundred years), he attempted to take the opposite path, i.e. not to trace the development from the individual portrait drawing to identity-free portrait photography using one example, but from it back to the portrait drawing: seventeen times, the indifference in Duchamp's likeness dissolved into interpretations. Whether this task was unusual for these street artists and perhaps even unsettled them is not the question here, but how did they see Duchamp? Did they try to visualise the face? How did they create a living face in the quasi-photo transfer? Did they discover something in it that Duchamp had hidden in the photo-thing?

Showing imagination was not part of their task, but rather creating similarity. Surprisingly, in each drawing lies a new accent: Duchamp's head, for example, was suddenly depicted slightly tilted, his lips smiling a little, as if he were listening and amused by what he was hearing. This is how he might have looked in reality. Then again, he looks a little sad or pensive (and indeed, Duchamp seems to have experienced a number of disappointing moments around 1912, as Rudolf Herz writes in his book ›Marcel Duchamp. Le Mystère de Munich‹ about this period. Did the Parisian street artist know about this?). Duchamp's forehead, which is not quite evenly symmetrical in his photo, was closely observed by some of the street artists and so strongly accentuated that it turns out to be an unsightly conspicuous feature. Or Duchamp suddenly looks dreamy, like a young Romantic, suffering like Goethe's alter ego ›Werther‹.

Perhaps it was his second, barely shown side that a street artist recognised - whether unconsciously or not – in Duchamp's face back then in Munich? Some others depict him as sporty, either with bulging cheeks that even shine out in colour, or with a sharp and strongly contoured jaw and thickened lips. Whether Duchamp had ever practised sport has been forgotten. Then again, the artist looks questioningly forwards or downwards and appears as well-dressed as a young up-and-coming banker. This face can also appear defiant with its mouth pursed or, to the contrary, with its mouth slightly drawn in, subtle, introverted and vulnerable. Anyone familiar with Duchamp's biography and his artistic intentions will be able to imagine both. Apparently, some of the street artists were good observers in this respect. Formally, they tried to apply their own skills with contoured or blurred strokes to create darkness, to introduce curved, crossed or vertical hatching according to the usual taste, or to adhere to the given chiaroscuro details in the photograph, for example by shading a quarter of the face but leaving it glowing in the light overall. At one point, a tiny aureole was even hinted at behind Duchamp's head.

One street artist seems to use his skills more skilfully than the other, but what they all have in common is the attempt to liven up an almost frozen image with minimal means. Their aim does not seem to be to create a resemblance, but to bring the sitter into the present. The seventeen attempts thus return Duchamp to us as a person who obviously intended to elude us viewers. Basically, however, the seventeen drawings are so different that the revitalised identity evaporates into non-identity. This fits in with Duchamp's preference for contradictions.

So perhaps Duchamp would have been quite happy for his face to be seen anew seventeen times by anonymous street artists around a century later. After all, a photographer like Hoffmann was also a »collaborator« on the photo thing. And finally, Duchamp explained in his Aspen lecture in 1957 that the viewer makes the work ... In this case, there were even seventeen who drew what they thought they saw. One recognises all the efforts of the street artists to breathe life into Duchamp's sterile photograph. This is precisely what makes it understandable as an early attempt at an identity-alienated readymade.

PHILIPP NORMAN JOHN

The self-portrait as a moment of liberation in Marcel Duchamp

A portrait photo, 17 unknown street painters of today and a biographical gap in the life of the artist Marcel Duchamp. In the meantime, Duchamp embodies one of the most influential positions of modernism. This tense starting point reveals aspects of an art-historical drama to which the Munich-based artist Rudolf Herz draws attention in his project, the results of which lead to this exhibition and are published here.

The location chosen by Rudolf Herz for his initiative was not chosen at random. For it was the city of Paris, the cradle of modern painting, which Marcel Duchamp had left in the summer of 1912 in order to distance himself from the disputes about the ›right‹ way of painting, which the Cubists and many other isms were claiming for themselves at the time. Duchamp was deeply involved in this scene. On the one hand, he had already sold paintings through the Salon d'Automne, on the other hand, his ›Nude Descending a Staircase‹ was rejected even by his friends, whereupon he removed the painting from the Salon des Indépendants himself. Apollinaire had called another of his nudes »extremely ugly«. That doesn't sound good, but in the context of the debate about contemporary painting at the time, it doesn't necessarily have to be meant disrespectfully, especially as the same author included Duchamp in his anthology ›Les Peintres Cubistes‹ and even ennobled him at the end with the sentence, »It will perhaps fall to an artist as free of aesthetic considerations and as concerned with energy as Marcel Duchamp to reconcile Art and the People.«[1] Incidentally, Duchamp was in love with the wife of his friend Francis Picabia and had had a child with a married woman ... So an invitation from a painter friend to Munich came at just the right time.

Duchamp distanced himself from the Parisian art scene, his private entanglements, Cubism, painting in general ... and found himself in Munich. In Duchamp's own words: »My stay in Munich was the scene of my complete liberation.«

Rudolf Herz surmises that Hoffmann's portrait must be a key to this decisive moment, because the self-portrait has always been regarded as a document of the artistic attitude of the person portrayed. Dürer's self-portrait from 1500 hanging in the Munich Pinakothek, which Herz referred to in his publication ›Marcel Duchamp. Le Mystère de Munich‹ (2012) and which is clearly identified as such by the artist through the inscription, is a good example of the role the self-portrait can play for the artist. Duchamp would have seen it at the time.

The question of mimesis is at the centre of the modern phenomenon of the independent artist portrait. This is not only to demonstrate an artistic ability, but also to achieve a credibility based on the scientific knowledge of the time. Following Leone Battista Alberti's treatises on art theory from 1435, the artist's portrait finds its foundation in the ancient myth of Narcissus: »Consequently I used to tell my friends that the inventor of painting, according to poets, was Narcissus, who was turned into a flower; for, as painting is the flower of all arts, so the tale of Narcissus fits our purpose perfectly. What is painting but the act of embracing by means of art, the surface of a pool?«[2]

The face in the mirror of the water surface as the cradle of painting! One could now argue: Hoffmann's portrait of Duchamp is not a self-portrait in the classical sense. But the notion that an object not made by the artist himself can carry an artistic statement can be found in Duchamp's readymades, which he conceived from this phase onwards in Munich. The question of the extent to which Duchamp's stage directions produced the indifferent expression, indeed the poker face of the photograph, is not known. Hoffmann's usual portraits of the time are in any case more conventional. The Duchamp portrait has something soldierly, even warlike about it. His features display an unemotional lack of intention. In the context of portrait photography at the time, a good decade before New Objectivity, it is a vehement gesture, a decision without a narrative context.

Over the course of several years, Rudolf Herz showed this strange-looking portrait of Duchamp to 17 street painters in Paris. They were commissioned by him to make drawings based on this photograph, each using their own means, their own artistic signature, which in French can be described with the beautiful term ›la patte‹, the paw. The result is 17 portraits that could hardly be more different. The graphic interpretations react like the mountain nymph Echo to the photographic portrait of the self-reflecting Narcissus. Without the ability to formulate themselves, they are reduced to merely reflecting the photographic image – distorted. But in doing so, they undermine the appearance of the objective, sober portrait, as if they wanted to turn the rejection of painting by the artist portrayed, which is reflected in the photographic image, into the opposite.

The criticism of the Platonic conception of art was that the portrait, as a mere duplication of nature, lacked imagination, fantasy and a higher capacity for cognition. For the aim is not only to create something resembling the portrayed, but to express the true image, more similar than merely that of the sitter's external physiognomy.

Duchamp's portrait is therefore to be understood as a memorandum, whose lack of context, inscriptions, clothing, location, facial expression, movement and mood are intended to indicate the artistic attitude. Explaining oneself through a portrait of oneself implies not least a reflection of one's inner self, symbolised by the reflection and thus the external appearance. The originality of the Narcissus myth for an ‚original' definition of portrait painting is repeated in the repeatedly asserted interrelationship between the genesis of portrait painting and the discovery of individuality. [3]

The linking of these two starting points in a common myth of origin is itself speculative, because it necessarily binds self-examination to self-knowledge. However, if all painting is a self-portrait of inwardness due to the expressiveness and handwriting of modernism, then it follows for Duchamp that one must turn back to the outside world if one wants to distance oneself from the reflection of this very inwardness. In other words, to turn back to one's surroundings, to direct attention back to the social, to that which is opposite the subject in individuation, that would be the »reconciliation of art with the people«, as Apollinaire hoped for from Duchamp's aesthetic lack of reservation.

Herz's work takes a critical look at Duchamp's deconstructive rejection of painting by tracing deconstruction back to its origins. The question posed by the 17 portraits of street painters could be: how can one give in to the urge to be artistically active if one simultaneously decides to stop doing so? A new concept is needed. A transformation. A new way of looking at the things you have done so far that have produced unsatisfactory results for you. It is difficult to say whether Duchamp was only looking for external confirmation or whether he was seeking intrinsic motivation in Munich. At the very least, the fact that he sought distance from Paris for this transformation suggests that he was more concerned with the latter, that he did not want to be influenced by negative or positive attention from critics or fellow artists. Whatever ... Perhaps it was simply the pain of an unfulfilled love that drove him away.

1) Quoted from: Daniels, Dieter: Duchamp und die Anderen. Der Modellfall einer künstlerischen Wirkungsgeschichte in der Moderne. Cologne 1992, p. 48.

2) Alberti, Leon Battista: La Pittura. Übers. Lodovico Domenichi, Venedig 1547, Sala Bolognese 1988, S.19.

3) Cf. Boehm, Gottfried: Bildnis und Individuum. Über den Ursprung der Portraitmalerei in der italienischen

RUDOLF HERZ

studied Art and History of Art in Munich, Oldenburg and Hamburg; scholar of the Villa Massimo, Rome (1995); winner of the competition for the ›Memorial to the Murdered Jews of Europe‹ (with Reinhard Matz); projects in public spaces (›Szeemann and Lenin Crossing the Alps‹, 2003) and exhibitions in Germany and abroad; honorary professor at the Academy of Fine Arts Munich.

ANTJE VON GRAEVENITZ

professor emeritus, taught general History of Art with a focus on the 20th/21st century at the University of Cologne (1989-2005) and lectured at the University of Amsterdam (1977-1988). She completed her doctorate in Munich in 1973 on Baroque ornamentation, but specialised in contemporary, anthropological, ephemeral and interdisciplinary topics.

PHILIPP NORMAN JOHN

completed his doctorate in 2016 on Hans Haacke and worked on participatory approaches in art and mediation; lecturer at the Berlin University of the Arts and the FU Berlin as well as the University of Potsdam; board member of the Bernhard Heiliger Foundation in Berlin, and since 2023 managing director of the Museum FLUXUS+ in Potsdam.

MARIE-JOSÉ SONDEIJKER

is co-founder and director of the art institute West Den Haag. She has collaborated with national and international artists on many exhibitions. Since 2007, the organization has been focussing on art that challenges viewers' conditioning and perception of art. West Den Haag is currently located in the former U.S. Embassy in the center of The Hague.

RUDOLF HERZ

studierte Kunst und Kunstgeschichte in München, Oldenburg und Hamburg. Stipendiat der Villa Massimo, Rom (1995), Preisträger im Wettbewerb für das ›Mahnmal für die ermordeten Juden Europas‹ (mit Reinhard Matz), Projekte im öffentlichen Raum (›Szeemann and Lenin Crossing the Alps‹, 2003) und Ausstellungen im In- und Ausland, Honorarprofessor an der Akademie der Bildenden Künste München.

ANTJE VON GRAEVENITZ

Professorin i. R., lehrte Allgemeine Kunstgeschichte mit dem Schwerpunkt 20./21. Jahrhundert an der Universität zu Köln (1989–2005) und dozierte an der Universität von Amsterdam (1977–1988). Sie promovierte 1973 in München über Barock-Ornamentik, spezialisierte sich aber auf zeitgenössische, anthropologische, ephemere und interdisziplinäre Themen.

PHILIPP NORMAN JOHN

promovierte 2016 über Hans Haacke und arbeitete zu partizipativen Ansätzen in Kunst und Vermittlung, Dozent an der Universität der Künste und der FU Berlin sowie der Universität Potsdam, Vorstandsmitglied der Bernhard-Heiliger-Stiftung in Berlin und seit 2023 Geschäftsführer des Museum FLUXUS+ in Potsdam.

MARIE-JOSÉ SONDEIJKER

ist Mitbegründerin und Leiterin des Kunstinstituts West Den Haag. Sie hat bei zahlreichen Ausstellungen mit nationalen und internationalen Künstlern zusammengearbeitet. Seit 2007 konzentriert sich die Organisation auf Kunst, die die Konditionierung und Wahrnehmung von Kunst durch den Betrachter herausfordert. West Den Haag befindet sich in der ehemaligen US-Botschaft im Zentrum von Den Haag.

IMPRESSUM / COLOPHON

Diese Publikation erscheint anlässlich der Ausstellung / This publication is released to accompany the exhibition:
Rudolf Herz. Marcel Duchamp. La Patte

museum Fluxus+, Schiffbauergasse 4f, 14467 Potsdam

West Den Haag, Lange Voorhout 102, 2514 EJ, Den Haag

West

Herausgeber / Editors: Philipp Norman John, Marie-José Sondeijker
Zeichnungen / Drawings: Amery, Bonno, Copperfield, Eduard, Linda Galic, Hoie, Jaffar, Idk, Dany Jim, Galina Konopitskaya, Les Satan, Majid, Mohai, O. Pirez Pertus, Stéphane Plouviez, Suilic
Texte / Texts: Antje von Graevenitz, Rudolf Herz, Philipp Norman John, Marie-José Sondeijker
Übersetzung / Translation: Christopher Robson

Gestaltung / Design: Horst Moser, independent medien-design, Munich
Reproduktionen / Reproductions: Hans Döring
Lithographie / Lithography: BayerMedia, Munich
Druck / Printed: Weber Offset, Munich
Projektmanagement / Project management: Lily von Wild / Kerber Verlag

Gefördert von / Supported by: Alligator. Art and Science e.V., Cologne University of Potsdam, Department of Arts and Media, Potsdam

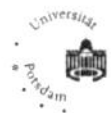

Vielen Dank an / Many thanks to Costantino Ciervo, Antje von Graevenitz, Andreas Köstler, Reinhard Matz, Francis Naumann, Matthias Reichelt, Julia Wahren

Kerber Verlag
Detmolder Straße 60
33604 Bielefeld
Germany
+49 521 950 08 10
+49 521 950 08 88 (F)
info@kerberverlag.com
kerberverlag.com

Kerber Publikationen werden weltweit vertrieben: / Kerber publications are distributed worldwide:

ACC Art Books
Sandy Lane
Old Martlesham
Woodbridge, IP12 4SD
UK
+44 1394 38 99 50
+44 1394 38 99 99 (F)
uksales@accartbooks.com
accartbooks.com

AVA Verlagsauslieferung AG
Centralweg 16
8910 Affoltern am Albis
Switzerland
+41 44 762 42 50
+41 44 762 42 10 (F)
avainfo@ava.ch

Artbook | D.A.P.
75 Broad Street, Suite 630
New York, NY 10004
USA
+1 (212) 627-1999
+1 (212) 627-9484 (F)
orders@dapinc.com
artbook.com

Zeitfracht Medien GmbH
Distribution
Germany
+49 711 7860 2254
service.zeitfracht.de

Die Deutsche Nationalbibliothek verzeichnet diese Publikation in der Deutschen Nationalbibliografie: dnb.de. / The Deutsche Nationalbibliothek lists this publication in the Deutsche Nationalbibliografie: dnb.de.

ISBN : 978-3-7356-0982-3
www.kerberverlag.com
Printed in Germany